THE MOTI MAHAL COOKBOOK

THE MOTI MAHAL
COOKBOOK
On the Butter Chicken Trail

Monish Gujral

PENGUIN BOOKS

PENGUIN BOOKS
Published by the Penguin Group
Penguin Books India Pvt. Ltd, 11 Community Centre, Panchsheel Park,
New Delhi 110 017, India
Penguin Group (USA) Inc., 375 Hudson Street, New York, New York
10014, USA
Penguin Group (Canada), 90 Eglinton Avenue East, Suite 700, Toronto,
Ontario, M4P 2Y3, Canada (a division of Pearson Penguin Canada Inc.)
Penguin Books Ltd, 80 Strand, London WC2R 0RL, England
Penguin Ireland, 25 St Stephen's Green, Dublin 2, Ireland (a division of
Penguin Books Ltd)
Penguin Group (Australia), 250 Camberwell Road, Camberwell, Victoria
3124, Australia (a division of Pearson Australia Group Pty Ltd)
Penguin Group (NZ), 67 Apollo Drive, Rosedale, North Shore 0632, New
Zealand (a division of Pearson New Zealand Ltd)
Penguin Group (South Africa) (Pty) Ltd, 24 Sturdee Avenue, Rosebank,
Johannesburg 2196, South Africa

Penguin Books Ltd, Registered Offices: 80 Strand, London WC2R 0RL,
England

First published by Penguin Books India 2009

Text copyright © Monish Gujral 2009
Photographs from the collection of Monish Gujral.

10 9 8 7 6 5 4 3 2 1

ISBN 9780143065920

Typeset in Sabon by Mantra Virtual Services, New Delhi
Printed at Gopsons Papers Ltd., Noida

A tradition to follow...
A culture to preserve...
A legacy to inherit...
To my children
Tanisha and Gunav

Contents

Acknowledgements

The first in the long list of people I want to thank are those who encouraged me to write *The Moti Mahal Cookbook* and helped make my first book a bestseller. I also want to include those who compelled me to provide the recipe for Moti Mahal's famous butter chicken in this book.

I want to thank my wife Sonal for standing by me and for her simplicity and grace; and my children, Tanisha and Gunav. I would not be the person I am without them.

I am grateful to my mother Rupa, who has been both mother and father to me after my father's demise, for keeping me on the right 'trail'.

Thanks are also due to my sister Anuradha Bhalla and my brother-in-law Dr Tarun Bhalla; Sachin, my right hand man; all my franchisees who have shared my dreams for Moti Mahal, particularly Pravin and Bela who have crossed the barrier to become close friends; my team at work, whom I fondly refer to as 'my cabinet', ably led by Suresh Mehra; and last but not the least, to all those who swear by Moti Mahal and whose loyalty has made it a legend.

Foreword

Monish Gujral is one of modern India's success stories. In my book, he is to Delhi and the rest of India what Rahul Akerkar and Moshe Shek are to Bombay: a restaurateur-chef who can cook everything on the menu of his popular chain of Moti Mahal restaurants, a businessman, a food writer, and a gourmet. I know him as restaurateur and friend; and, I cannot as yet decide whether I like his food better or his friendship. Probably his friendship, because Moti Mahal food—its butter chicken, maa ki dal, roti and kulfi, I can get in 72 cities around India; but not Monish's genuinely hearty and delightful Punjabi company. For that, I have to wait till he visits Mumbai. Then it is friendship and food, a double whammy, as we sit talking and eating late into the night.

I am always amazed at how he adds to the number of Moti Mahals each time we meet. I cannot remember how many they were at last count. But today there are 72 across India, and by 2009 there will be 110, after which he intends taking the brand abroad – to Australia, New Zealand, Dubai, South East Asia. It is a good idea; and God bless, because the number of imitation Indian, Pakistani and Bangladeshi restaurants like the Moti Mahals there are around the world, claiming to serve the asli butter chicken and maa ki dal, is really not funny.

But that, I am afraid, is the cross Monish has to bear for his family's simplicity in business and its large heartedness. His grandfather Kundan Lal Gujral, a handsome man from Peshawar known as much for his dhaba food as for his Pathani suits, handlebar moustache, fondness for good whisky and a closeness to Indira Gandhi, is responsible for this state of affairs.

He made Moti Mahal famous all over Delhi, but neglected to register the brand as his family's proprietary trademark. As a result, there are more Moti Mahals today between Delhi and Vancouver than the late Kundal Lal would care to know.

Happily, Monish stepped in at the right time and registered the brand. Having reclaimed the title that was rightfully the family's, he has made Moti Mahal into the brand it is today, and is proudly taking it forward. Kundan Lal's post-Partition dhaba had become a 400-seat restaurant in Daryaganj by 1948, with regulars like Pandit Jawaharlal publicly extolling the virtues of the restaurateur's signature dish—his tandoori chicken. Maulana Azad is reputed to have said that just as they visited Agra and did not leave without seeing the Taj Mahal, nobody should come to Delhi and go away without having at least one meal at Moti Mahal. But, really, the restaurant was not the elite, fine dining eatery then that it is today. It was more a mom-and-pop shop. That was when Monish stepped into the picture in 1983.

The story goes that he had just passed out of junior college and accepted a summer job in a five star hotel bookshop. Kundan Lal imperiously asked his grandson, 'How much are they paying you?' Monish replied, 'Rs. 600.' The old man magnanimously offered, 'Come and work in my kitchen and I will pay you Rs. 700.' That, I think, was the moment Moti Mahal's fortunes changed. For Monish took up the offer. And he trained under Kundan Lal who was an outstanding cook. But Monish simultaneously studied commerce, he did hotel management, and when his father and Kundan Lal's only son passed away early at 49, Monish stepped into his shoes.

Winds of change swept through Moti Mahal then, Monish standardized the food, he created mother recipes that are common to all 72 Moti Mahal restaurants, he set up a corporate office at Gurgaon, and a big school of master chefs to train juniors and accompany them to new restaurants in the chain where they hold hands in the kitchen until the new Moti Mahal, too, finds its feet.

In Delhi, Moti Mahal is a social hotspot. Everybody dines here, from Nehru's great granddaughter, Priyanka Gandhi Vadra to visiting heads of state, film stars, politicians who disagree violently in Parliament, celebrity sportsmen, multinational CEOs, Indian captains of industry...

The restaurant business in India is an exciting challenge and Monish Gujral, who is intrigued by the romance of adventure, has picked up this gauntlet. In taking Moti Mahal across India, he recognized the potential of setting up shop in the spanking new granite, chrome and glass shopping malls everywhere. 'Restaurants make malls attractive destinations and malls assure restaurants the footfalls they need to stay in business,' he reasoned. And he has grown in time; he is a jet-setting businessman, a popular food writer, a man-about-town, a gourmet who cooks at home for the wife and children. But, I am happy to say he has kept Moti Mahal's food the same. Kundan Lal's signature dishes remain; some additions were made, but people blindly come and order the butter chicken, maa ki dal and roti. 'It is difficult to tell them to try anything different,' Monish said. I know, every time we meet he tries to interest me with a different order. I yield because he is my friend. And also because I have had in his absence, the week before, the butter chicken, maa ki dal and roti!

Mark Manuel
Editor, *Bombay Times*

Author's Note

On the butter chicken trail

From the very beginning, I have cherished and treasured the history and glamour attached to Moti Mahal. As a child, I remember going to the restaurant with my grandfather and father occasionally, and seeing a film star or celebrity dining there. I would boast about this the following day, feeling elated when my classmates envied me. Little did I know then that my early childhood fascination with Moti Mahal was to become a lifelong passion; a passion to set up one Moti Mahal restaurant in every city of India, to be visible globally. I dreamt with open eyes; the only dream I have ever seen is of and for Moti Mahal.

Moti Mahal, the restaurant that gave the world the celebrated butter chicken, the tandoori chicken and the dal makhani, has been capturing hearts since it was started over 85 years ago in Peshawar in 1920. Inspiring patrons to shower it with lavish praise, Moti Mahal has, since 1947, been one of the most important fixtures on the culinary map of Delhi and in subsequent years, India. It is believed that Maulana Azad, then the minister for education, government of India, told the Shah of Iran, who was on an official visit to India that 'Going to Delhi and not visiting Moti Mahal is like going to Agra and not visiting the Taj Mahal.' Moti Mahal's butter chicken became so popular that Delhi was nicknamed 'the butter chicken capital'. Today all the Moti Mahal restaurants together sell over 100,000 butter chickens a year

As the story goes, young Kundan Lal, in the early 1920s created the tandoori chicken only to impress his mentor, the owner of the eatery he worked for in Peshawar, then in undivided India. Following his employer's request to serve him something light and not greasy, a novel idea struck him. He marinated chicken with some yogurt and spices and lowered it into the hot clay oven, the tandoor, by piercing an iron wire into the marinated bird. (There were no skewers, as in those days the tandoor was only used to bake breads such as naan, paratha and roti.) What came out was a tandoori chicken and the rest is history. Impressed with the new invention, the dish was soon added to the menu. Word spread and people flocked to taste the new dish. The restaurant, then known as a dhaba, became a landmark called Moti Mahal.

Partition followed shortly forcing many to flee from their homelands and find refuge in distant places. Kundan Lal's fate was similar. Affluent enough by then to afford a plane ride to Delhi, he fled with his family—his mother Maya Devi, wife Prakash Devi, and his young son Nand—and some decent savings. Initially, he found refuge in a camp, and set off immediately on a mission to find a suitable place to start his own little restaurant. He soon spotted a property in Daryaganj, then a prime marketplace in Delhi and bargained a deal for himself to start the first Moti Mahal restaurant in India in 1947. News about the cuisine spread fast and attracted the glitterati and the who's who of Delhi to Moti Mahal. It became a club for people to interact while savouring their favourite dishes.

There are only a handful of chefs in the world who have been credited with the creation of a single dish let

Kundan Lal Gujral receiving the Worldwide Tourism Award in 1987

alone an entire cuisine. Kundan Lal was one of those rare chefs who gave the world a whole new cuisine called Tandoori cuisine.

It was in the kitchens of Moti Mahal that butter chicken was also created. As the old saying goes, 'necessity is the mother of all inventions'. The tandoori chicken and the tikka would get dry hanging besides the hot tandoors all day long in those days, in the absence of refrigerators. To overcome such wastage, Kundan Lal again pondered and introduced the butter gravy. The combination of tandoori chicken and butter gravy proved to be a masterstroke and once again the taste buds of the old and the young, men and women alike, were tantalised by this delectable invention. Even today when I hear children say

Kundan Lal Gujral with Jawaharlal Nehru

that butter chicken is their favourite dish it makes me proud to be associated with Moti Mahal. It makes me proud when leaders like Renuka Choudhuri say, 'When we travel abroad and are invited to Indian homes for a meal, and they serve butter chicken, they say, "We have tried our best, but surely it is not of the same standard as Moti Mahal's." Moti Mahal has set a bench mark and maintained its culinary excellence all these years.'

As Kundan Lal Gujral's grandson, I was always groomed to join and further the Moti Mahal legacy. But my romance with Moti Mahal only really began when I finished school. A bet I made with a friend then made all the difference in my life and landed me where I am today. It was a bet to outdo him in getting a job for the summer while we waited for the Class 12 results to be declared, and university to begin. It was a fashion statement in those days to announce at a party that one was employed and

Lal Bahadur Shastri with Kundan Lal Gujral at Moti Mahal

earning money. I didn't want to be left behind.

While searching for a suitable job, I was given a lucrative offer by my grandfather to work at Moti Mahal, Daryaganj. Greedily, I accepted the offer to work four hours a day on a whopping salary of Rs. 700 per month. It was a princely salary for a 17-year-old in the early 1980s.

The very next day, I reported for the job, dressed in my finest clothes, as befitted the restaurant owner's grandson. To my utter surprise I was sent home, only to report later in a pair of jeans and a casual t-shirt. To my horror, I was summoned to the kitchen where I was instructed to observe the operations for the next 15 days, constantly under the gaze of my grandfather, who was probably in his early 60s at the time. With a distinctively Punjabi, well-built, dominating physique, chunky, framed glasses and a well-tended, signature handlebar moustache, my grandfather made his presence felt. He was to become the first great influence in my career.

Initially baffled and broken-hearted at this apparent snub, trying to reconcile myself to my fate, I sweated it out in the unfriendly atmosphere of the vast kitchen. Gradually it turned into my playground with the chefs as my best friends. However, it was in the hot, steamy environs of the kitchens that I underwent some of the most important experiences of my life. Learning the finer nuances of cooking from my grandfather, undergoing rigorous kitchen training, I started to understand the importance of preparing food the right way. By then I knew that food had power: power to inspire, delight, attract, impress and to please; and that a chef was at once a technologist, an artist, a tasks-man, a team leader and a creator. Later, during my term at the catering institute, working with some of the finest chefs, I realized that each of them had some other passion. One wanted to be an

Indira Gandhi enjoying a meal at Moti Mahal

artist, the other was a failed musician and the third a philosopher and they brought considerable artistry to their roles as master chefs. Cooking is a performing art: one has to be an artiste first and then a chef.

That summer working in the Moti Mahal kitchens ignited a life-long romance with food for me. After completing three years at Delhi university studying business management, I joined the Institute of Hotel Management, Pusa, Delhi, confident and armed with the

Monish Gujral with A.P.J. Abdul Kalam at Rashtrapati Bhavan to present the Moti Mahal qawwali CD and his first cookbook

training and culinary skills learnt in the kitchens of Moti Mahal and ready to face the challenges of the hotel management course. I took special classes in food handling, salads, butchery, soups, basic knife work, chopping tons and tons of vegetables, learning about the different cuts of mutton, and so on. What people may not understand about professional cooking, I had already learnt on the job at Moti Mahal: it is not about the best recipe, the most innovative presentation, the creative blend of ingredients, flavours and colours; in the real business of food it is consistency and quality all the way. I have always upheld the 4Ps formula taught at Moti Mahal:

The famous artist Satish Gujral feasts on the Moti Mahal Tandoori Chicken

product, place, price and people. The first is about the quality and consistency of the food served at the restaurant. Second, the success of the restaurant depends on its location. The third is the pricing strategy, depending on your target customers, and last but not the least, the people around whom the business revolves, so it is essential to have perfect public relations.

With my hotel management degree in hand, I was ready now to face the challenges of the real food business and set out on a journey I called the Tandoori Trail.

One day I was called upon by the Indian Express to demonstrate cooking butter chicken at the British Council, Delhi at the invitation of Mr Marsden, then the director of the Council. I accepted the invitation keenly enough. Mr Marsden's words, after taking the first bite, still echo in my mind: 'The bird has truly migrated.'

Today, CTM (chicken tikka masala) is the national dish of Britain. What is CTM? It is just a derivative of butter chicken. When Foreign Secretary Robin Cook showcased the chicken tikka masala as the symbol of multicultural Britain, he only succeeded in turning the boneless dish into a major bone of contention.

By declaring chicken tikka masala 'Britain's true national dish' because 'it is a perfect illustration' of the

Qawwali singers at a Moti Mahal Nite

way Cool Britannia 'absorbs and adapts external influences', Cook cooked up a racial row with serious political overtones, and unwittingly triggered a culinary controversy in the home of the chicken tikka. 'Chicken tikka is an Indian dish,' Cook declared in a speech. 'The masala was sauce added to satisfy the desire of the British people to have their meat served in a gravy.' The Foreign Secretary's advert for 'an open and inclusive society' immediately raised the hackles of subcontinental gastronomes who have made Britain the country of over 9,000 curry restaurants (compared with a measly ten in 1955).

Although the fleet of Indian and Bangladeshi cooks in the UK modified our butter gravy by including Campbell's tomato sauce and adding some spices, not only to suit the British palate, but also to find a shortcut to our butter gravy made with tomato purée in a time consuming and laborious process, the fact still remains that it is out and out a derivative of the tandoori chicken and butter gravy made in Moti Mahal since 1920.

Because of the phenomenal global demand for Indian cuisine, hundreds of restaurants serving Indian food have been established worldwide. Ready-to-eat Indian curries and food that were unheard of a few years ago are fast emerging as the new magic words in the kitchens across the globe. The ready-to-eat packed Indian food market grew to $20 million in revenue in 2004, with a growth rate of over 35 per cent per year.

In such a scenario I know that it is not foolish or futile to dream of a worldwide presence for Moti Mahal. I hope the Tandoori Trail will take Moti Mahal to the far corners of the globe traversed by the butter chicken, chicken tikka, dal makhani, et al and make it as popular abroad as it is in India. This book is another step in that direction. It is an attempt to take Moti Mahal's cuisine into the homes of lovers of Tandoori food. I invite you, the reader, to take this little piece of the Moti Mahal experience home with you. Read it, try the recipes over and over again, mark your favourites, savour the magic of Moti Mahal.

Bon appétit!

Monish Gujral
New Delhi
December 2008

Introduction

The tandoor or the clay oven was introduced to India by the Central Asians, during the Mughal invasion. In those days the tandoor was used as a sanjha choolha, or common oven for baking bread, and was the central point of the village where the women would gather, bringing their dough to bake into bread (tandoori roti or naan).

I have been more partial to kabab recipes in this book, particularly as kababs have become a very important part of the weight watchers diet chart, being devoid of excess oil and other saturated fats. This in turn has led to a specialization in kabab cooking, and owing to a considerable amount of experimentation, tandoori cooking has come a long way since my grandfather Mr Kundan Lal first made it.

In Arabic the word 'kab' refers to a turning movement and 'cabob' means a piece of roasted or grilled meat or vegetable. Any combination of these words could have given rise to the word 'kabab'.

Whether it is a rack of lamb, a tandoori chicken, a fish tikka or any other kabab, the mastery of tandoori cooking lies in the succulence of the meat being cooked with its juices sealed in. When meat is plunged into a hot tandoor where the temperature is about 600°C, the outside is instantly roasted and forms a seal, which helps retain the juices during the cooking process that takes place at around 180°C. One must keep the following points in mind while mastering the art of tandoori cooking

- The meat should not be overcooked, as it tends to become hard and dry.
- The marinade must be a thick paste to coat the item being cooked thoroughly. When using yogurt as part of a marinade it should be drained of excess liquid for about 2 hours.
- The spices, which play an important role in a perfect tandoori dish should be appropriately pounded to bring out their aromas.
- As temperature is the key to tandoori cooking remember to spread the coal evenly at the base of the tandoor to ensure an even temperature
- When yogurt or cream is a part of a marinade, add some flour or gram flour to avoid curdling.

Basic Recipes

COOKING IN A TANDOOR

A tandoor is a clay oven heated by a wood or charcoal fire and can attain very high temperatures. It was originally used to bake breads. The dough was slapped on to the sides of the oven and baked. Kundan Lal Gujral, the founder of the Moti Mahal Restaurant, was the first to use a tandoor to cook chicken, fish, meat and vegetables.

Tandoors that use gas or electricity are now available in the market in various sizes for the home kitchen. A regular oven, preheated to 180°C, can be used if a tandoor is not available. Place a tray under the skewers to catch the drippings. The food can also be grilled under a hot electric grill or over a charcoal one.

- Fix the food to be cooked on to skewers, 1" apart, and place in a preheated, moderate-hot tandoor for the time stipulated in the recipe.
- Remove the skewers from the oven and point them downwards over a bowl for 2-3 minutes to drain off excess liquid.
- Baste the food with oil, ghee or melted butter as given in the recipe, invert the skewers into the tandoor, to ensure even heating, and roast again for the time mentioned in the recipe.
- If using a regular oven or grill, rotate the skewers to ensure that all sides of the food are evenly cooked.

HUNG YOGURT

Makes: 1 cup

3 cups yogurt

- Hang yogurt in a muslin bag for 2 hours to drain, with a bowl underneath to catch the drippings.
- The drained yogurt is called hung yogurt.

TOMATO PURÉE

Makes: 1½ cups

1 kg ripe, red tomatoes
3 tbsp oil
1 small onion, chopped
A pinch of salt

- Chop tomatoes roughly and place in a pan over moderate heat. Add oil, onion and salt and cook till tomatoes are tender and oil floats to the surface.
- Remove from heat and press tomatoes through a strainer to remove seeds and skin.
- Store purée in the refrigerator for up to 1 week.

CASHEW NUT-CHEESE PASTE

Makes: 2 tbsp

2½ tsp cashew nuts
1 tsp grated processed Cheddar cheese
1 tbsp milk
1 tbsp cream

- Grind all ingredients to a smooth paste.

Variations:
- To make 3 tbsp **Cashew Nut-Cheese-Mint Paste,** add 1 tbsp of chopped mint leaves to the ingredients and grind.
- To make 1 tbsp **Cashew Nut Paste,** grind 2 tsp cashew nuts with 2 tsp milk.

GREEN CHILLI-CORIANDER PASTE

Makes: about 7 tsp

6-8 green chillies, seeded and chopped
100 gms coriander leaves

- Grind ingredients together to a smooth paste, gradually adding about 3 tbsp of water.

RED CHILLI PASTE

Makes: about 1 tbsp

2 tsp red chilli powder
½ tsp white vinegar

- Combine ingredients in a small bowl with 1 tsp water.

GARAM MASALA POWDER

Makes: about 500 gms

200 gms cumin seeds
350 gms black peppercorns
11 black cardamoms
2½ tbsp green cardamoms
12 tbsp (60 gms) coriander seeds
4 tbsp cloves
20 x 1" sticks cinnamon
2 tbsp mace powder (javitri)
7 bay leaves (tej patta)
6 tbsp ginger powder (saunth)
2 nutmegs (jaiphul)

- Heat a dry frying pan and gently toss each ingredient separately over moderate heat, till fragrant, to remove excess moisture.
- Combine all ingredients, cool and grind to make a fine powder.
- Sift and store in an airtight container.

TANDOORI MASALA

Makes: about 1 kg

400 gms coriander seeds
400 gms cumin seeds
100 gms black cumin seeds (shah jeera)
250 gms rose petals
150 gms mace (javitri)
150 gms cinnamon
100 gms black peppercorns
60 gms star anise (badian)
2½ tbsp green cardamoms
12 black cardamoms
6 tbsp cloves
3 tbsp nutmeg powder (jaiphul)

- Heat a dry frying pan and gently toss each ingredient separately over moderate heat, till fragrant, to remove excess moisture.
- Combine all ingredients, cool and grind to a fine powder.
- Sift and store in an airtight container.

AROMATIC SPICE MIX

Makes: 500 gms

250 gms mace (javitri)
250 gms green cardamoms

- Combine both ingredients and grind to make a fine powder.
- Sift and store in an airtight container.

CORIANDER CHUTNEY

A BLEND OF FRESH CORIANDER

Makes: about 1¼ cups

1 cup (200 gms) coriander leaves, roughly chopped
3 tbsp mint leaves, roughly chopped
2 tbsp chopped ginger
6 green chillies, seeded and chopped
Juice of 1 lime
½ tsp cumin seeds, crushed
1 tsp salt

- Grind all ingredients together to make a smooth paste, adding a little water if required.

MINT CHUTNEY

THE FAMOUS MOTI MAHAL CHUTNEY

Makes: about 2¼ cups

1 cup chopped mint leaves
2 cups chopped coriander leaves
2 tbsp chopped ginger
6 green chillies seeded and chopped
2 tbsp pomegranate seed powder (anardana)
1 cup (250 gms) yogurt
1 tsp salt
Juice of 1 lime

- Grind all ingredients except yogurt, salt and lime juice to make a smooth paste, gradually adding up to 4 tsp of water.
- Mix in yogurt, salt and lime juice.

PEANUT CHUTNEY

Makes: about ½ cup

100 gms peanuts, skinned and roasted
2 green chillies, roughly chopped
2 tbsp lime juice
1 tsp chopped ginger
3 cloves garlic, chopped
1 tbsp groundnut oil
½ tsp salt

- Grind all ingredients together to make a paste of a granular consistency, gradually adding about 5 tbsp of water.
- Refrigerate till ready to serve.

LASUN AUR MIRCH CHUTNEY

GARLIC AND CHILLI CHUTNEY

Makes: about ½ cup

40 gms dried red chillies
2 tbsp garlic paste
4 tsp lime juice
1 tbsp refined oil
½ tsp salt

- Soak chillies in hot water for 30 minutes.
- Drain and grind with remaining ingredients, gradually adding about 5 tbsp of water to make a semi-smooth paste.
- Allow chutney to stand for 2-3 hours before serving.

AAM KI CHUTNEY

Mango Chutney

Makes: about 1 kg

1½ kg raw, green mangoes
1 cup grated onions
3½ tbsp ginger paste
1½ tbsp garlic paste
1 kg sugar
1 tbsp red chilli powder
1 tbsp garam masala powder
½ tsp cinnamon powder
1 cup white vinegar
2 tsp salt
½ cup seedless raisins (kishmish), soaked in water
1 tbsp melon seeds (magaz), soaked in water

- Wash mangoes, peel and chop, discarding seeds.
- Place onions and ginger paste in a muslin cloth and squeeze out juice. Discard residue, mix juice with garlic paste and set aside.
- Place mangoes and sugar in a heavy-based pan and cook over moderate heat for 12-15 minutes, stirring occasionally.
- Add onion-ginger-garlic mix and spice powders and cook, stirring frequently, till the mixture attains the consistency of jam.
- Stir in vinegar and salt and cook for 2-3 minutes.
- Remove from heat and set aside till cool.
- Drain raisins and melon seeds, dry on a kitchen towel and sprinkle into chutney.
- Store in a jar for 2-3 days to mature before use. The chutney will stay for about 10 days.

TIL AUR TAMATER KI CHUTNEY

SESAME AND TOMATO CHUTNEY

Makes: about ½ cup

4 tsp whole Bengal gram (kala chana)
1 tsp + 2 tbsp groundnut oil
1 cup chopped onions
½ tsp red chilli powder
½ tsp turmeric powder
A pinch of asafoetida powder (hing)
2 tbsp sesame seeds (til)
1 cup chopped tomatoes
1 tsp salt

Tempering:

2 tbsp refined oil
5 dried red chillies
20 sprigs curry leaves
½ tsp mustard seeds

- Wash gram and soak in water overnight. Drain and rinse in several changes of water.
- Heat 1 tsp of oil in a pan and sauté gram over moderate heat for 5-6 minutes, tossing frequently. Remove pan from heat and set aside.
- Heat 2 tbsp of oil in a pan, add onions and sauté over moderate heat, till golden brown.
- Stir in spice powders and sesame seeds and stir-fry for a few minutes. Add gram, tomatoes and salt and cook for 10 minutes. Remove from heat and allow to cool.
- Grind to make a paste and spoon into a bowl.
- Heat oil for tempering in a small pan and add remaining ingredients for tempering. When mustard seeds splutter, mix contents of pan into chutney and serve.

Relishes and Soups

IRANI RAITA

IRANIAN RELISH

Serves: 4

4 cups yogurt, whisked
5 tbsp honey
3 tbsp seedless raisins (kishmish), chopped
½ tsp white pepper powder
1 tsp salt
½ tsp cumin seeds, roasted and powdered
450 gms cucumber, peeled and finely chopped

Garnish:

1 tsp chopped coriander leaves

- Combine all ingredients, except cucumber and garnish, in a bowl and whisk till well blended.
- Fold in cucumber, garnish with coriander leaves and serve chilled.

PALAK SHORBA

Cumin and Burnt Garlic Spinach Soup

Serves: 6-8

500 gms spinach
1 tbsp olive oil
1 tsp chopped garlic
2 tbsp butter
1 tsp cumin seeds
2 tbsp refined flour (maida)
5 tsp chopped ginger
½ tsp black peppercorns
4 bay leaves (tej patta)
1 tsp salt
A pinch of white pepper powder
7 cups vegetable stock (see note)

- Pluck spinach leaves and wash thoroughly in several changes of water. Chop fine and set aside.
- Heat oil in a small pan and sauté garlic over low heat for 3-4 minutes till dark brown. Drain and set aside.
- Melt butter in a pan over low heat and add cumin seeds. When they splutter, stir in flour. Cook over low heat, stirring continuously, till it starts to sizzle.
- Blend in spinach, garlic and ginger and sauté for a few minutes.
- Add peppercorns and bay leaves, and give it a stir.
- Mix in salt, white pepper and vegetable stock and simmer for 15-20 minutes.
- Strain stock into a fresh pan. Grind residue to a fine purée, and pour into stock.
- Place pan over moderate heat and simmer for about 6 minutes.
- Remove from heat and serve hot.

The Moti Mahal Cookbook

Note: To make vegetable stock, chop 10 French beans, 3 carrots, 2 onions, 2 potatoes and a small piece of cabbage and pressure-cook for 5 minutes with about 7 cups of water. Cool, strain and use.

RICE SOUP

Serves: 2

2 tbsp refined oil
1½ tsp sliced onion
1 tbsp chopped carrot
1 tbsp chopped baby corn
1 tbsp chopped broccoli
1 tsp chopped coriander leaves
1 tsp salt
1¾ cups rice water (starch)
1 tbsp coconut milk (medium strength)

Garnish:

2 tbsp boiled rice
¾ tsp chopped spring onion

- Heat oil in a pan and add onion. Stir-fry over moderate heat, till brown.
- Add all ingredients except coconut milk and garnish. Bring to boil, lower heat and simmer for 4-5 minutes.
- Just before serving, heat through and remove pan from heat.
- Pour in coconut milk. Do not reheat soup after adding coconut milk as it may curdle.
- Taste and adjust seasoning. Garnish with boiled rice and spring onions and serve.

Chicken

TANDOORI CHICKEN

Serves: 3-4

1 chicken without skin (600-700 gms), kept whole
Refined oil for basting

First marinade:

1½ tbsp lime juice
1 tsp red chilli powder
1 tsp salt

Second marinade:

½ cup yogurt
1 tbsp garlic paste
1 tbsp ginger paste
½ tsp black salt (kala namak)
1 tsp garam masala powder
½ tsp dried fenugreek leaf powder (kasuri methi)

- Wash chicken inside and outside thoroughly and pat dry. Make 2 deep incisions into chicken flesh on breast and drumsticks.
- Combine all ingredients for first marinade. Rub into chicken and set aside for about 1 hour.
- Combine all ingredients for second marinade. Rub into chicken and set aside for at least 3 hours.
- Fix chicken on to a skewer and roast in a preheated tandoor, regular oven or grill, as given on p. 3 for 5-6 minutes initially, and 3-4 minutes after draining and basting with oil.
- Slip chicken off skewer, joint it and serve with onion rings and lime wedges.

MURGH MAKHANI

BUTTER CHICKEN FOR THE STRONG HEARTED

Serves: 3-4

1 ready-cooked tandoori chicken, jointed (see p. 21)

Makhani gravy:

2 tbsp refined oil
1 medium-sized onion, chopped
4 medium-sized, ripe, red tomatoes, chopped
1 tsp salt
1 tbsp ginger-garlic paste
1 tbsp red chilli powder
1 tbsp garam masala powder
1 tsp cumin powder
2 tbsp butter
Scant ½ cup fresh double cream

Garnish:

2 green chillies, seeded and chopped
1 tbsp chopped coriander leaves
1 tbsp fresh cream

- Heat oil in a large pan and sauté onion over moderate heat for a few seconds, till soft.
- Add tomatoes and salt and simmer, stirring occasionally, till oil floats to the surface.
- Strain sauce into a fresh pan and place it over moderate heat. Mix in ginger-garlic paste and spice powders.
- Immerse chicken into gravy and stir for 3-4 minutes, to coat chicken thoroughly.
- Add butter and stir till it melts. Pour in cream, give it a quick stir and remove pan from heat immediately.
- Garnish with green chillies, coriander leaves and a swirl of cream.

ACHARI MURGH TIKKA

PICKLED CHICKEN

Serves: 2

350 gms boneless chicken
Melted butter for basting

First marinade:

½ tsp ginger paste
½ tsp garlic paste
2 tbsp lime juice
¾ tsp salt

Second marinade:

1 tbsp yogurt
1½ tsp red chilli powder (degi mirch)
1 tsp garam masala powder
¾ tsp chaat masala (commercial)
¾ tsp meat masala (commercial)
1 tsp cumin powder
¾ tsp dried fenugreek leaves (kasuri methi)
¾ tsp black salt (kala namak)
1 tbsp pickle paste (commercial)
1 tbsp malt vinegar

- Wash chicken, pat dry and cut into 3" pieces.
- Combine all ingredients for first marinade. Rub into chicken and set aside for about 1 hour.
- Combine all ingredients for second marinade. Rub into chicken and set aside for 2-3 hours.
- Fix chicken pieces on to skewers, 1" apart, and roast in a tandoor, regular oven or grill as given on p. 3 for 6-7 minutes initially, and 3-4 minutes after draining and basting with melted butter.
- Slip tikka off skewers and serve hot with mint chutney (see p. 8).

LAHSOONI MURCH

Garlic Chicken

Serves: 2

350 gms boneless chicken
Melted butter for basting

First marinade:

¾ tsp ginger-garlic paste
½ tsp salt
2 tbsp lime juice

Ground to a smooth paste:

3 spinach leaves, boiled and drained
1 tsp chopped green chillies
1 tsp garlic paste

Second marinade:

2-3 green chillies, seeded
1 tsp garlic paste
A pinch of salt
1 tsp white pepper powder
¾ tsp green cardamom powder
3 tbsp cashew nut-cheese paste (see p. 5)
1 tbsp cream
1 egg, whisked

- Wash chicken, pat dry and cut into 3" pieces.
- Combine all ingredients for first marinade. Rub into chicken and set aside for about 1 hour.
- Combine spinach paste with remaining ingredients for second marinade. Rub into chicken and set aside for 2-3 hours.
- Fix chicken pieces on to skewers, 1" apart, and roast in a preheated tandoor, regular oven or grill, as given on p. 3 for 5-6 minutes initially, and 3-4 minutes after

draining and basting with melted butter.
- Slip chicken off skewers and serve hot with mint chutney (see p. 8).

AFGHANI MURGH

AFGHAN-STYLE CHICKEN

Serves: 3-4

1 chicken (about 600 gms) without skin, cut into 8 pieces

First marinade:

¾ tsp ginger-garlic paste
2 tbsp lime juice
1 tsp salt

Second marinade

3 tbsp cashew nut-cheese paste (see p. 5)
1 tbsp cream
1 egg, whisked

- Wash chicken and pat dry.
- Combine all ingredients for first marinade. Rub into chicken and set aside for about 1 hour.
- Combine all ingredients for second marinade. Rub into chicken and set aside for 2-3 hours.
- Fix chicken pieces on to skewers, 1" apart, and roast in a preheated tandoor, regular oven or grill, as given on p. 3 for 5-6 minutes initially, and 3-4 minutes after draining and basting with oil.
- Slip chicken off skewers and serve hot with mint chutney (see p. 8).

PUDINA MURGH TIKKA

MINT-FLAVOURED CHICKEN

Serves: 2

350 gms boneless chicken
Melted butter for basting

First marinade:

¾ tsp ginger-garlic paste
2 tbsp lime juice
½ tsp salt

Second marinade:

¾ tsp white pepper powder
¾ tsp green cardamom powder
3 tbsp cashew nut-cheese-mint paste (see p. 5)
1 egg, whisked

- Wash chicken, pat dry and cut into 3" pieces.
- Combine all ingredients for first marinade. Rub into chicken and set aside for about 1 hour.
- Combine all ingredients for second marinade. Rub into chicken and set aside for 2-3 hours.
- Fix chicken pieces on to skewers, 1" apart, and roast in a tandoor, regular oven or grill as given on p. 3 for 6-7 minutes initially, and 3-4 minutes after draining and basting with melted butter.
- Slip tikka off skewers and serve hot with mint chutney (see p. 8).

The Moti Mahal Cookbook

KESARI DUM MURGH

Slow-Cooked Saffron Chicken

Serves: 3-4

1 chicken without skin (about 700 gms), cut into 8 pieces
1 cup ghee
1 small onion, sliced
4 green cardamoms
2 cloves
2 x 1" sticks cinnamon
2 tbsp coriander powder
1½ tsp garam masala powder
1 tsp salt
2 tbsp garlic paste
1²/₃ cups yogurt
½ cup lukewarm milk
5 tbsp ground almonds
10-12 saffron strands (kesar)
Stiff dough made with 1½ cups refined flour (maida) and ¼ cup water

- Wash chicken and pat dry.
- Heat ghee in a pan and sauté onion over moderate heat, till golden brown. Add whole spices, give it a stir and remove from heat.
- Drain onion and spices and grind to make a fine paste.
- Return drained ghee to pan and place over moderate heat. Add spice powders, salt, garlic paste, yogurt and milk. Stir and cook for a few minutes.
- Add chicken and cook over low heat till half-done.
- Stir in onion paste, ground almonds and saffron strands.
- Cover pan and seal lid with dough. Place pan on a tava or griddle over very low heat to cook on dum for 5-8 minutes, till chicken is tender.
- Remove from heat and serve hot.

MURGH BADAM PASANDA

CHICKEN ESCALOPE WITH ALMONDS

Serves: 4

700 gms boneless chicken
4 tbsp ghee
1½ tbsp almonds, sliced
5 green cardamoms
8 cloves
1 medium-sized onion, chopped
2 large tomatoes, chopped
1½ tsp red chilli powder
¾ tsp black pepper powder
1 tbsp refined flour (maida)
1 litre chicken stock (see note)
¾ tsp mace powder (javitri)
10-15 saffron strands (kesar) dissolved in 1 tbsp milk

Marinade:

2½ tbsp ginger paste
1 cup hung yogurt (see p. 4)
1¼ tbsp garlic paste
1 tsp salt

Garnish:

4 tbsp chopped coriander leaves

- Wash chicken and pat dry. Cut chicken into 3" pieces. Place chicken pieces between 2 damp plastic sheets or cling film and flatten gently with a wooden mallet.
- Rub ginger paste for marinade over chicken.
- Whisk yogurt in a large bowl and mix in garlic paste and salt. Rub into chicken and set aside for about 1 hour.
- Heat 1 tbsp ghee in a small pan and fry almonds till brown. Drain and set aside.

- Heat half the remaining ghee in a large frying pan or griddle and place chicken pieces in it. Fry over moderate heat, turning the pieces occasionally, till half-cooked. Remove from heat and set aside.
- Pour remaining ghee into another pan and place over moderate heat. Sauté cardamoms and cloves till they splutter. Add onion and stir-fry till golden brown.
- Blend in tomatoes, chilli powder, black pepper powder, flour and stock. Simmer over moderate heat till gravy is thick.
- Add chicken to pan and cook, stirring occasionally, for about 10 minutes.
- Sprinkle in mace powder and saffron milk. Stir for 1 minute and remove from heat.
- Serve garnished with coriander leaves.

Note: To make chicken stock, place about 500 gms of chicken in 3 litres of water, bring to boil, lower heat and simmer till reduced to 1 litre. Strain and use.

PARDA TANDOORI MURGH

Pastry-Covered Tandoori Chicken

Serves: 2-3

1 marinated, uncooked tandoori chicken, cut into 4 pieces
(see p. 21)
½ cup cream

Parda (*pastry*):

1 tbsp sugar
½ cup warm milk
3 drops vetiver essence (kewda)
1 cup refined flour (maida) + extra for dusting
1 tsp salt
2 tbsp melted butter + extra for greasing
2 egg yolks, whisked

- Roast chicken in a preheated moderate-hot tandoor, regular oven (180°C) or grill for 5 minutes. Remove from oven or grill and set aside.
- Dissolve sugar in warm milk, add vetiver and stir.
- Sift flour and salt into a mixing bowl.
- Pour in sweetened, flavoured milk and knead well. Set aside for 10 minutes.
- Add melted butter to dough and knead again.
- Divide dough into 2 portions and roll them into balls. Dust with flour and set aside for 5 minutes.
- Lightly grease the base of 2 round ovenproof dishes with extra butter.
- Roll the balls of dough into discs the size of the dishes on a lightly floured surface and prick all over lightly with a fork.
- Divide tandoori chicken between the dishes. Sprinkle with cream and cover each dish with a dough disc.
- Press dough down firmly along edges of dish to seal.

The Moti Mahal Cookbook

- Brush dough with egg yolk.
- Bake in oven preheated to 150°C for 10-12 minutes, till crust is golden brown.
- Cut open the pastry and serve the chicken along with a portion of the pastry.

KADHAI MURGH

CHICKEN IN A TOMATO GRAVY

Serves: 2-3

1 chicken without skin (600 gms), cut into 8 pieces
2 tbsp refined oil
4 tbsp ginger-garlic paste
1 bay leaf (tej patta)
2 black cardamoms
3 green cardamoms
3 cloves
2 blades mace (javitri)
1" stick cinnamon
1½ tsp garam masala powder
¾ tsp cumin powder
¾ tsp red chilli powder (degi mirch)
1 tsp salt
1 large onion, chopped
1 medium-sized green bell pepper, chopped
1 medium-sized tomato, chopped
2 tbsp butter
⅓ cup cream

Garnish:
½ tbsp chopped coriander leaves

- Wash chicken and pat dry.
- Heat oil in a pan and add ginger-garlic paste and bay leaf. Sauté over moderate heat for a few seconds.
- Add whole spices and sauté, tossing continuously for about 1 minute.
- Sprinkle in spice powders and salt and give it a stir.
- Add onion and bell pepper and stir for 2-3 minutes.
- Blend in tomato and sauté for 2-3 minutes.
- Add chicken pieces and ½ cup of water and mix gently.

- Cook over moderate heat for about 10 minutes, till chicken is tender.
- Mix in butter and stir for 2-3 minutes.
- Fold in cream, stir for 1 minute and remove from heat.
- Serve hot, garnished with coriander leaves.

BHARWAN TANGRI KABAB

STUFFED CHICKEN DRUMSTICKS

Makes: 16 kabab

16 chicken drumsticks
Melted butter for basting

Filling:

2 tbsp refined oil
1 tbsp chopped cashew nuts
300 gms minced chicken
1 tsp salt
1 tsp garam masala powder
4 tbsp chopped coriander leaves
A pinch of saffron strands

First marinade:

¾ tsp ginger-garlic paste
2 tsp lime juice
1 tsp white pepper powder
A pinch of salt

Second marinade:

200 gms processed Cheddar cheese, grated
1 egg white, whisked
1¾ cups cream
1 tsp ginger-garlic paste
¼ tsp green cardamom powder
¼ tsp mace powder (javitri)
1 tbsp chopped coriander leaves

- Wash chicken drumsticks and pat dry. Make a slit along the bone with a sharp knife, and scrape some of the flesh off the bone to make a pocket. Turn drumsticks over and make 2 slits in the flesh.
- Heat oil for filling in a pan. Add cashew nuts and

mince and sauté over moderate heat, till mince turns white.

- Sprinkle in remaining ingredients for filling and stir-fry till mixture is completely dry. Remove from heat and set aside till cool.
- Divide filling into 16 equal portions and fill pockets in chicken drumsticks.
- Combine all ingredients for first marinade. Rub into chicken and set aside for about 1 hour.
- Place cheese and egg white for second marinade in a tray and gradually mix between your palms.
- Pour in cream and continue to mix till mixture is smooth. Add remaining ingredients for second marinade and mix well.
- Place drumsticks in tray and rub in marinade. Set aside for at least 2 hours.
- Fix drumsticks on to skewers, 1" apart, and roast in a preheated tandoor, regular oven or grill, as given on p. 3 for 5-6 minutes initially, and 3-4 minutes after draining and basting with melted butter.
- Slip chicken off skewers and serve hot with mint chutney (see p. 8).

MURGH BEMISAL

Chicken with Minced Lamb

Serves: 2-3

600 gms boneless chicken
Scant 1 cup refined oil
2 black cardamoms
2 green cardamoms
3 cloves
2 blades mace (javitri)
1" stick cinnamon
1 bay leaf (tej patta)
1 tbsp ginger-garlic paste
2 medium-sized onions, chopped
¾ tsp garam masala powder
¾ tsp cumin powder
¾ tsp meat masala (commercial)
¾ tsp red chilli powder (degi mirch)
1 tsp salt
150 gms minced lamb
¾ cup tomato purée
2 tbsp butter
½ cup cream

Garnish:

2 tbsp chopped coriander leaves

- Wash chicken and pat dry. Cut chicken into 8 pieces and set aside.
- Heat oil in a heavy-based pan and toss in whole spices and bay leaf. Stir for 2-3 minutes over moderate heat.
- Mix in ginger-garlic paste and sauté for a few seconds. Add onions and sauté till golden brown.
- Sprinkle in spice powders and salt and stir for a few seconds. Mix in mince and sauté till it turns white.

- Add chicken, mix well and cook for 7-8 minutes, till chicken is almost tender.
- Blend in tomato purée, cover pan and cook for 3-4 minutes.
- Add butter and stir for 2 minutes.
- Fold in cream and remove from heat.
- Serve hot, garnished with coriander leaves.

MURGH SHAHI KORMA

CHICKEN IN A CASHEW NUT GRAVY

Serves: 2

350 gms boneless chicken
2 tbsp refined oil
4 tbsp ginger-garlic paste
1 bay leaf (tej patta)
2 black cardamoms
3 green cardamoms
3 cloves
2 blades mace (javitri)
1" stick cinnamon
1 tsp salt
1½ tsp white pepper powder
2 medium-sized onions, chopped
100 gms cashew nuts, ground
1 tbsp butter
⅓ cup cream

- Wash chicken and pat dry. Cut chicken into 2" cubes and set aside.
- Heat oil in a pan and add ginger-garlic paste and bay leaf. Sauté over moderate heat for a few seconds and add whole spices. Sauté for about 1 minute.
- Add salt, white pepper and onions and stir-fry for 2-3 minutes.
- Blend in cashew nuts and sauté till mixture is smooth.
- Stir in chicken pieces and cook for about 10 minutes, till chicken is tender.
- Add butter and stir till blended.
- Pour in cream and stir for a few seconds.
- Remove from heat and serve hot.

ADRAKI MURGH KABAB

GINGER-FLAVOURED CHICKEN KABAB

Serves: 5-6

1 kg boneless chicken breasts

First marinade:

1 tbsp green chilli paste
2 tsp white pepper powder
1½ salt
4 tbsp ginger paste
4 tsp malt vinegar

Second marinade:

1 cup hung yogurt (see p. 4)

Garnish:

2 tsp ginger juliennes

- Wash chicken and pat dry. Cut chicken into 3" cubes.
- Combine all ingredients for first marinade. Rub into chicken and set aside for about 30 minutes.
- Whisk yogurt in another bowl. Rub into chicken and set aside for about 1 hour.
- Fix chicken pieces on to skewers, 1" apart, and roast in a preheated tandoor, regular oven or grill, as given on p. 3 for 8-10 minutes initially, and 3-4 minutes after draining excess liquid.
- Slip kababs off skewers and serve hot, garnished with ginger juliennes.

Mutton and Lamb

BADAMÉ SHAMI KABAB

LAMB KABAB WITH ALMONDS

Serves: 4

1 kg minced lamb
2 tsp husked Bengal gram (chana dal)
5 dried red chillies
5 green chillies, kept whole
5 black cardamoms
5 bay leaves (tej patta)
5 x 1" sticks cinnamon
10 cloves
3 eggs, whisked
2 tsp salt
¼ cup slivered almonds
Refined oil for deep-frying

- Boil mince with Bengal gram, red and green chillies, whole spices and 10 cups of water till water evaporates.
- Remove red chillies and whole spices and discard. Grind mince to make a smooth paste.
- Add eggs and salt and knead well. Mix in almonds.
- Divide mixture into 16 even-sized balls and shape into flat, round cutlets.
- Heat oil in a kadhai or wok and deep-fry cutlets in batches over moderate heat till crisp and brown on all sides. Drain and place on kitchen paper to absorb excess oil.
- Serve hot.

SEEKH KABAB MAKHANI MASALA

LAMB KABAB IN A RICH TOMATO GRAVY

Serves: 4

Kabab:

500 gms minced lamb
1 egg, whisked
1 medium-sized onion, finely chopped
2 green chillies, finely chopped
1½ tsp red chilli powder
1 tsp chopped ginger
1½ tsp garam masala powder
1 tsp salt
Refined oil for basting

Gravy:

2 tbsp refined oil
1 medium-sized onion, chopped
2 tbsp ginger-garlic paste
1 tsp cumin powder
1 tsp coriander powder
1 tsp turmeric powder
2 tsp red chilli powder
1 tsp garam masala powder
1 tsp salt
2 green chillies, sliced
1⅓ cups tomato purée
1 tbsp lime juice
2 tbsp butter
½ cup fresh double cream

Garnish:

1 tbsp chopped coriander leaves

Kabab:

- Combine all ingredients for kababs, except oil for basting, in a bowl.

- Divide mixture into 16 portions and shape into balls. Moisten your hands and fix the balls on to skewers, shaping them into 2" long kababs along the length of the skewers.
- Roast kababs in a preheated tandoor, regular oven or grill, as given on p. 3 for 7-8 minutes initially, and 3-4 minutes after draining and basting with oil.
- Slip kababs off skewers and set aside.

Gravy:
- Heat oil in a kadhai or wok. Add onion and sauté over moderate heat till golden brown.
- Stir in ginger-garlic paste and sprinkle in spice powders and salt. Stir-fry for a few minutes and carefully lower in kababs. Stir gently for 3-4 minutes.
- Blend in green chillies, tomato purée and lime juice and stir for a few minutes.
- Add butter, and as it melts, pour in cream and remove from heat.
- Stir to blend and serve hot garnished with coriander leaves.

Variation: The seekh kababs can also be served as a snack without the gravy, garnished with chopped coriander leaves and lime wedges.

GOSHT LABABDAR

Lamb in a Rich Creamy Gravy

Serves: 2

300 gms boneless lamb
4 tbsp refined oil
2 black cardamoms
3 green cardamoms
3 cloves
2 blades mace (javitri)
1" stick cinnamon
1 bay leaf (tej patta)
1½ tbsp ginger-garlic paste
1 large onion, chopped
1½ tsp red chilli powder (degi mirch)
1½ tsp white pepper powder
¾ tsp dried fenugreek leaves (kasuri methi)
½ cup tomato purée
¾ tsp chopped green chillies
1 small green bell pepper, sliced
1 tsp salt
1 tbsp butter
½ cup cream

Garnish:

2-3 green chillies, sliced

- Wash meat, pat dry and cut into 2" cubes. Set aside.
- Heat oil in a heavy kadhai or wok. Add whole spices and bay leaf and stir over moderate heat for 2-3 minutes.
- Stir in ginger-garlic paste and sauté for 2-3 minutes. Add onion, and fry, stirring continuously, till golden brown.
- Mix in meat, spice powders and fenugreek leaves and cook for a few minutes, stirring well to coat meat.

- Add tomato purée and green chillies and cook, stirring frequently till oil floats to the surface.
- Pour in 3 cups of water and mix well.
- Cover pan and cook for 20-30 minutes, stirring occasionally, till meat is tender and semi-dry.
- Mix in bell pepper and salt and sauté for 2-3 minutes over high heat.
- Add butter and stir till it melts. Pour in cream, give it a stir and remove from heat.
- Serve hot garnished with sliced green chillies.

DAL GOSHT

LAMB WITH LENTILS

Serves: 2

300 gms lamb on the bone, cut into 2" pieces
½ cup refined oil
2 black cardamoms
3 green cardamoms
3 cloves
2 blades mace (javitri)
1" stick cinnamon
1 bay leaf (tej patta)
1½ tbsp ginger-garlic paste
2 medium-sized onions, chopped
1½ tsp garam masala powder
1½ tsp cumin powder
¾ tsp meat masala (commercial)
¾ tsp coriander powder
¾ tsp red chilli powder (degi mirch)
¾ tsp dried fenugreek leaves (kasuri methi)
²⁄₃ cup tomato purée
2 green chillies, chopped
²⁄₃ cup (150 gms) husked black gram (urad dhuli)
1 tsp salt
2 tbsp butter
2 tbsp fresh cream

Garnish:

2 tbsp chopped coriander leaves

- Wash meat, pat dry and set aside.
- Heat oil in a heavy kadhai or wok. Add whole spices and bay leaf and stir for 2-3 minutes over moderate heat.
- Stir in ginger-garlic paste and sauté for 2-3 minutes. Add onions and fry, stirring continuously, till golden brown.

- Sprinkle in spice powders and fenugreek leaves and give it a stir.
- Add meat and stir till well coated with spices.
- Mix in tomato purée and green chillies and cook, stirring frequently till oil floats to the surface.
- Pour in 3 cups of water and mix well. Cover pan and cook for 20-30 minutes, stirring occasionally, till meat is tender.
- Wash dal and place in another pan with 1 cup of water.
- Cook dal over moderate heat for 9-10 minutes, till grains are still firm and slightly under-cooked. Check periodically to ensure the grains are not overcooked.
- Drain off excess water and add dal to meat with salt. Sauté for 2-3 minutes.
- Add butter and stir till it melts.
- Pour in cream and stir for 1-2 minutes over low heat.
- Remove from heat, garnish with coriander leaves and serve hot.

GOSHT PASANDA MASALA

Mutton Escalope in a Tomato Gravy

Serves: 2

300 gms boneless mutton
Refined oil for basting

First marinade:

150 gms unripe papaya
1¾ tsp ginger-garlic paste
1 tsp red chilli powder mixed with 1 tsp water
1 tsp salt
2 tsp white vinegar
1 tbsp refined oil

Second marinade:

²/₃ cup hung yogurt, whisked (see p. 4)
2 tbsp garam masala powder
1 tsp red chilli powder mixed with 1 tsp water
1 tsp salt
1 tbsp white pepper powder
2 tbsp lime juice

Gravy:

2 tsp refined oil
2 medium-sized onions, finely chopped
¾ tbsp ginger-garlic paste
2 black cardamoms
3 green cardamoms
3 cloves
2 blades mace (javitri)
1 bay leaf (tej patta)
¾ tsp garam masala powder
¾ tsp cumin powder
¾ tsp chaat masala (commercial)
1½ tsp red chilli powder (degi mirch)
1 tsp salt
1 medium-sized tomato, puréed

1 tbsp green chilli-coriander paste (see p. 5)
2 medium-sized green bell peppers, sliced
2 tsp lime juice
2 tbsp butter
½ cup cream

Garnish:

2 tbsp chopped coriander leaves

- Wash meat, pat dry and cut into 8 pieces. Place meat pieces between 2 damp plastic sheets or cling film and flatten gently with a wooden mallet.
- Combine all ingredients for first marinade. Rub into meat and set aside for about 2 hours.
- Squeeze meat pieces between your hands to remove excess moisture.
- Whisk all ingredients for second marinade. Rub into meat and set aside for about 3 hours.
- Fix meat pieces on to skewers, 1" apart, and coat with marinade left in bowl. Roast in a preheated tandoor, regular oven or grill, as given on p. 3 for 10 minutes initially, and 3-4 minutes after draining and basting with oil. Set aside.

Gravy:
- Heat oil in a kadhai or wok. Add onions and sauté over moderate heat till golden brown.
- Mix in ginger-garlic paste, whole spices and bay leaf and sauté for 2-3 minutes.
- Sprinkle in spice powders and salt. Add cooked meat and sauté for about 5 minutes.
- Mix in tomato, green chilli-coriander paste, bell peppers and lime juice and stir for 3-4 minutes.
- Add butter and stir for about 2 minutes. Mix in cream and remove from heat.
- Garnish with coriander leaves and serve hot.

CHATPATTÉ PUDINA CHAAMP

TANGY LAMB CHOPS

Serves: 4

1 kg lamb chops
Refined oil for basting
2 tbsp lime juice

First marinade:

1 tsp cumin powder
1 tbsp white pepper powder
2 tsp garam masala powder
5 tsp lime juice

Second marinade:

4 tsp cream
¾ cup hung yogurt, whisked (see p. 4)
1¼ cups mint chutney (see p. 8)
2 tsp maize flour (makki ka atta)
1 tbsp garlic paste
1 tbsp ginger paste
3 tbsp unripe papaya paste
1 tsp dried fenugreek leaves (kasuri methi)
1½ tsp salt

- Wash chops and pat dry.
- Combine all ingredients for first marinade. Rub into chops and set aside for about 1 hour.
- Mix cream, yogurt, mint chutney and maize flour. Add remaining ingredients for second marinade and whisk till well blended. Rub into chops and set aside for 2-3 hours.
- Fix chops on to skewers, 1" apart, and roast in a preheated tandoor, regular oven or grill, as given on p. 3 for 10 minutes initially, and 5 minutes after draining and basting with oil.
- Slip chops off skewers and sprinkle with lime juice.

KASURI GOSHT KABAB

Fenugreek-Flavoured Lamb Kabab

Serves: 4

1 kg boneless leg or shoulder of lamb
Refined oil for basting

First marinade:

3 tbsp ginger-garlic paste
3 tbsp white vinegar
2 tbsp red chilli powder
1 tsp black pepper powder
1½ tsp salt

Second marinade:

3 tbsp cream
3 tbsp grated processed Cheddar cheese
1 tsp garam masala powder
1 tsp cumin powder
A few saffron strands
½ tsp dried fenugreek leaf powder (kasuri methi)

Garnish:

2 tbsp chopped coriander leaves

- Wash meat, pat dry and cut into 3" cubes.
- Combine all ingredients for first marinade. Rub into meat and set aside for about 2 hours.
- Combine all ingredients for second marinade. Rub into meat and set aside for about 1 hour.
- Fix meat pieces on to skewers, 1" apart, and roast in a preheated tandoor, regular oven or grill, as given on p. 3 for about 10 minutes initially, and about 5 minutes after draining and basting with oil.
- Slip meat off skewers and serve hot, garnished with coriander leaves, and lime wedges on the side.

SEEKH KABAB GILAFI

LAMB KABAB WITH A VEGETABLE COATING

Serves: 8

Kabab:

1 kg minced lamb
3 tbsp ginger paste
200 gms brown onion paste (see note)
6 green chillies, seeded and minced
1 tbsp garam masala powder
2 tsp red chilli powder
2 tsp salt
2 tbsp refined oil
100 gms processed Cheddar cheese, grated

Coating:

1 egg, whisked
1 medium-sized onion, finely chopped
1 medium-sized green bell pepper, finely chopped
1 medium-sized tomato, seeded and finely chopped

Melted butter for basting

- Combine all ingredients for kababs, mixing thoroughly. Squeeze out any excess moisture.
- Combine all ingredients for coating, except butter and set aside.
- Divide kabab mix and coating into 16 equal portions.
- Shape kabab mix into balls. Moisten your hands and fix the balls on to skewers, shaping them into 2" long kababs along the length of the skewers. Smear coating over kababs.
- Roast kababs in a preheated tandoor, regular oven or grill, as given on p. 3 for 10-15 minutes initially, and 2-3 minutes after draining and basting with melted butter.

The Moti Mahal Cookbook

- Slip kababs off skewers and serve hot with onion rings and mint chutney (see p. 8).

Note: To make brown onion paste, deep-fry 2 medium-sized finely chopped onions till golden brown. Drain thoroughly and grind to a paste with about 2 tbsp of water.

SPICY LAMB STEAKS

Serves: 2-3

8 lamb steaks, 2"x 2"
Refined oil for basting

Marinade:

1 medium-sized onion, minced
²/₃ cup hung yogurt, whisked (see p. 4)
100 gms unripe papaya
1 tbsp garlic paste
1 tbsp green chilli paste, seeds discarded
1 tbsp poppy seeds (khus-khus), powdered
1 tbsp garam masala powder
1 tsp salt

- Wash steaks and pat dry.
- Combine all ingredients for marinade. Rub into meat and set aside for 2-3 hours.
- Fix steaks on to skewers, 1" apart, and roast in a preheated tandoor, regular oven or grill, as given on p. 3 for 8-10 minutes initially, and 3-4 minutes after draining and basting with oil.
- Slip steaks off skewers and serve hot with mint chutney (see p. 8).

PASANDA KABAB

Spicy Lamb Escalope

Serves: 3-4

1 kg boneless lamb
Refined oil for basting

First marinade:

150 gms unripe papaya
1½ tsp salt
1 tsp white pepper powder
2 tbsp ginger-garlic paste

Second marinade:

1 egg white, whisked
1¼ cups cream
1 tsp garam masala powder
2½ tbsp ground cashew nuts
½ tsp green cardamom powder
1 tbsp seeded, chopped green chillies

- Wash meat and pat dry. Cut meat into 3" pieces. Place them between 2 damp plastic sheets or cling film and flatten gently with a wooden mallet.
- Combine all ingredients for first marinade. Rub into meat and set aside for about 2 hours.
- Combine egg white, cream and garam masala in a deep tray and mix till well blended. Add remaining ingredients for second marinade and mix well. Rub into meat and set aside for 2 hours.
- Fix meat pieces on to skewers, 1" apart, and roast in a preheated tandoor, regular oven or grill, as given on p. 3 for 10 minutes initially, and 5 minutes after draining and basting with oil.
- Slip pasanda off skewers and serve hot with mint chutney (see p. 8).

Seafood

GOAN FISH CURRY

Serves: 3-4

500 gms fish fillets (any firm, white fish)
3 tbsp refined oil
6 green cardamoms
2 sprigs curry leaves
4-5 green chillies, slit
2 tsp chopped ginger
1 tbsp chopped garlic
1 medium-sized onion, chopped
½ tsp turmeric powder
2½ cups medium-strength coconut milk
1 tsp salt

- Wash fish thoroughly and pat dry.
- Heat oil in a kadhai or wok and add cardamoms, curry leaves, green chillies, ginger and garlic. Stir-fry over moderate heat for 1 minute.
- Add onion and sauté till translucent.
- Stir in turmeric and fish fillets and sauté for 7-10 minutes.
- Pour in coconut milk and salt and bring to boil over moderate heat, stirring continuously. Reduce heat to low and simmer for 4-5 minutes, stirring continuously.
- Spoon curry into a bowl and serve hot with hot steamed rice.

MACHCHI MUSALLAM

Spicy Baked Fish

Serves: 2-3

2 red snappers (750 gms each), kept whole
⅔ cup refined oil

Marinade:

3 tbsp ginger-garlic paste
¾ tsp turmeric powder
1 cup hung yogurt (see p. 4)
2 tbsp lime juice
2 tsp coriander powder

Gravy:

1 large onion, chopped
2 medium-sized tomatoes, chopped
1 tbsp red chilli powder
1 tbsp cashew nut paste (see p. 5)
1 tsp garam masala powder
1 tsp salt

Garnish:

4 tbsp chopped coriander leaves

- Clean fish and wash thoroughly. Pat dry and make light incisions in the flesh on both sides at 1" intervals.
- Combine all ingredients for marinade in a large plate. Rub evenly into fish and set aside for 1 hour.
- Heat oil in a large frying pan and fry fish, one at a time, over moderate heat on both sides, till golden brown. Drain and set aside. Reserve any marinade in the plate.
- Add onion to pan and sauté till translucent.
- Mix in remaining ingredients for gravy and stir-fry

for a few minutes, sprinkling in a few drops of water occasionally to prevent burning.

- Stir in reserved marinade, cover pan and cook over moderate heat for 3-4 minutes.
- Transfer fish to an ovenproof dish and spoon gravy over them.
- Cover dish and cook for about 35 minutes in an oven preheated to 180°C.
- Garnish with coriander leaves and serve hot with a tossed green salad.

DHANIA POMFRET TANDOORI

CORIANDER-FLAVOURED TANDOORI POMFRET

Serves: 4

4 pomfret (300-350 gms each)
Refined oil for basting

First marinade:

1 cup (200 gms) chopped coriander leaves
4 green chillies, seeded and chopped
1 tbsp ginger juliennes
1 tsp salt
6 cloves garlic, crushed
2 tbsp lime juice

Second marinade:

2 cups hung yogurt (see p. 4)
2 tbsp coriander powder
1 tbsp black peppercorns, crushed
1 tbsp white vinegar
2 tsp black salt (kala namak)
½ tsp salt
2 tbsp ginger-garlic paste
2 tsp red chilli powder

- Clean fish, wash thoroughly and pat dry. Make light incisions in the flesh on both sides at 1" intervals.
- Combine all ingredients for first marinade. Rub into fish and set aside for about 1 hour.
- Combine all ingredients for second marinade. Rub into fish and set aside for about 2 hours.
- Fix fish on to skewers, 1" apart, and roast in a preheated tandoor, regular oven or grill, as given on p. 3 for about 8 minutes initially, and 2-3 minutes after draining and basting with oil.
- Slip fish off skewers and serve hot with mint chutney (see p. 8).

TANGY FISH FRY

Serves: 8

1 kg fish fillets (any firm, white fish)
2¼ cups refined oil
1½ tsp chaat masala (commercial)

Marinade:

1½ tsp salt
1½ tbsp lime juice

Batter:

2 tsp ajwain
1½ tsp white pepper powder
1½ tsp red chilli powder
1½ tsp turmeric powder
1 cup gram flour (besan)
2 tbsp ginger-garlic paste
¼ cup white vinegar

- Wash fish thoroughly and pat dry. Prick fish all over with a sharp fork.
- Rub salt and lime juice over fish and set aside for about 30 minutes.
- Combine all ingredients for batter in a large bowl. Immerse fish in batter, ensuring the pieces are well coated and set aside for about 30 minutes.
- Heat oil in a kadhai or wok. Deep-fry fish in batches over moderate heat, till cooked through and golden brown. Drain and place on kitchen paper to absorb excess oil.
- Sprinkle chaat masala over fish and serve accompanied with lime wedges.

TANDOORI TROUT

Serves: 3-4

3 trouts (250 gms each), kept whole
Melted butter for basting

First marinade:

1½ tsp salt
1 tsp yellow chilli powder
1½ tsp ginger-garlic paste
1½ tsp white vinegar

Second marinade:

1⅓ cup hung yogurt (see p. 4)
½ tsp ginger-garlic paste
½ tsp ajwain
1 tsp garam masala powder
2 tbsp mustard oil
½ tsp turmeric powder

- Clean fish, wash thoroughly and pat dry. Make 3-4 deep incisions across each fish.
- Combine all ingredients for first marinade. Rub into fish and set aside for about 30 minutes.
- Combine all ingredients for second marinade, except oil and turmeric, in a large bowl.
- Place oil in a small pan over low heat and add turmeric. Cover pan and heat for 2 minutes. Pour into bowl containing second marinade and mix till well blended. Rub into fish and set aside for 2 hours.
- Squeeze excess moisture from fish. Fix fish on to skewers, 1" apart, and roast in a preheated tandoor, regular oven or grill, as given on p. 3 for about 10 minutes initially, and 2-3 minutes after draining and basting with oil.
- Slip fish off skewers and serve hot with mint chutney (see p. 8).

TANDOORI LOBSTER – 1

Serves: 2-3

750 gms lobster
Melted butter for basting

First marinade:

1 tbsp ginger-garlic paste
1 tbsp red chilli paste (see p. 6)
1 tsp salt
2 tsp white vinegar
2 tsp refined oil

Second marinade:

1 heaped cup (250 ml) hung yogurt, whisked (see p. 4)
½ tsp ginger-garlic paste
1 tsp red chilli paste
1 tsp salt
½ tsp ajwain
1 tsp garam masala powder
2½ tbsp mustard oil

- Remove shell from lobster, retaining its tail. Wash lobster flesh thoroughly and pat dry.
- Combine all ingredients for first marinade. Rub into lobster flesh and set aside for about 1 hour.
- Whisk hung yogurt with remaining ingredients for second marinade. Rub into lobster flesh and set aside for 2 hours.
- Squeeze excess moisture from lobster flesh.
- Fix lobster flesh on to skewers, 1" apart, and roast in a preheated tandoor, regular oven or grill, as given on p. 3 for about 10 minutes initially, and 2-3 minutes after draining and basting with melted butter.
- Slip lobster flesh off skewers and serve hot with mint chutney (see p. 8).

TANDOORI LOBSTER – 2

Serves: 4

4 medium-sized lobsters
Refined oil for greasing lobster shells
Melted butter for basting

First marinade:

4 tsp ginger paste
4 tsp garlic paste
½ tsp ajwain
½ cup malt vinegar
1½ tsp salt

Second marinade:

1 cup hung yogurt (see p. 4)
1 tsp white pepper powder
1 egg, whisked
4 tbsp grated cottage cheese (paneer)
3 tbsp gram flour
4 tbsp mustard oil
1 tsp red chilli paste (see p. 6)

Garnish:

4 lettuce leaves, shredded
1 medium-sized tomato, sliced
1 medium-sized onion, sliced in rings

- Cut each lobster into half and remove flesh from shell.
- Clean lobster flesh and remove the vein. Wash lobster flesh and pat dry.
- Wash lobster shells and dry. Dip shells into hot oil, drain and set aside.
- Combine all ingredients for first marinade. Rub into lobster flesh and set aside for about 1 hour.
- Whisk yogurt in a large bowl and mix in remaining ingredients for second marinade. Add lobster flesh to

bowl and mix to coat lobsters thoroughly with marinade. Set aside for about 3 hours.

- Fix lobster flesh on to skewers, 1" apart, and roast in a preheated tandoor, regular oven or grill, as given on p. 3 for about 5 minutes initially, and 2-3 minutes after draining and basting with butter.
- Slip lobster flesh off skewers and arrange in the shells.
- Garnish with shredded lettuce, tomato slices and onion rings and serve hot.

DAHI MAHI MACHCHI

FISH IN A YOGURT GRAVY

Serves: 3-4

700 gms pomfret fillets
2 tbsp refined oil
1 tbsp mustard seeds
10 curry leaves
1 medium-sized onion, chopped
2 tsp chopped garlic
2 medium-sized tomatoes, chopped
½ tsp turmeric powder
1 tsp red chilli powder
1 tsp cumin powder
1 tsp coriander powder
1 cup yogurt, whisked
1 tsp salt

Marinade:

½ tsp salt
½ tsp turmeric powder
3 tbsp lime juice

Garnish:

2 tbsp chopped coriander leaves

- Wash fish thoroughly and pat dry.
- Combine ingredients for marinade. Rub into fish and set aside for 20 minutes.
- Heat oil in a heavy-based frying pan and fry fish in batches over moderate heat till golden brown. Drain and set aside.
- Add mustard seeds and curry leaves to pan and when they splutter, add onion and garlic.
- Sauté over moderate heat till onion is translucent.
- Mix in tomatoes and cook, stirring frequently, till oil

floats to the surface.

- Sprinkle in spice powders, give it a stir and add yogurt and salt. Bring to boil, stirring continuously. Lower heat and simmer for about 7 minutes, stirring frequently.
- Slip fish into gravy and simmer for another 5 minutes, stirring gently.
- Arrange fish on a serving dish, spoon gravy on top and garnish with coriander leaves.

TAVA MACHCHI

PAN-FRIED FISH

Serves: 4

Gravy:

¼ cup ghee
2 tsp garlic paste
1 tsp coriander powder
½ tsp red chilli powder
2 green chillies, chopped
1 tbsp ginger juliennes
½ tsp dried fenugreek leaves (kasuri methi)
1 tsp salt
3 medium-sized tomatoes, chopped

Fish:

500 gms fish fillets (any firm, white fish)
¼ cup ghee
¾ tsp ajwain
1 small onion, chopped
1 tsp chopped ginger
2 green chillies, chopped
½ tsp red chilli powder
½ tsp coriander powder

Garnish:

½ tsp garam masala powder
2 tsp chopped coriander leaves

- Heat ghee for gravy in a kadhai or wok. Add garlic paste and sauté over moderate heat for a few minutes.
- Add remaining ingredients for gravy and cook till gravy thickens, stirring occasionally.
- Remove from heat and set aside.
- Wash fish thoroughly and pat dry.
- Heat ghee for fish on a large tava or griddle and fry

fish over moderate heat till half-cooked. Push fish
pieces to sides of tava.

- Sprinkle ajwain in the centre of tava and fry for a few
  seconds.
- Add onion and fry till translucent.
- Mix in remaining ingredients for fish and move fish
  into centre. Stir gently for a few minutes to coat fish
  with spices.
- Stir in gravy and cook till gravy is dry, stirring
  occasionally.
- Sprinkle garam masala and coriander leaves over fish.
  Remove from the heat and serve hot.

MACHCHI TIKKA MASALA

Fish Kabab in a Rich Tomato Gravy

Serves: 2-3

The British Foreign Secretary, Sir Robin Cook, while addressing a think tank in London in April 2001, claimed that murgh tikka masala was one of Britain's national dishes. This led to great speculation regarding the origin of this awesome, delicious dish. A majority indicated that it was derived from the butter chicken, created by Moti Mahal's Kundan Lal Gujral, almost 60 years ago.

I took the liberty of reinventing the dish by substituting fish for the chicken and the result was phenomenal, as you would taste after trying my recipe below.

500 gms boneless sole, cut into 3" cubes
1 tbsp lime juice
2 tbsp gram flour (besan)
Refined oil for basting
1 tbsp chaat masala (commercial)

First marinade:

2 tbsp lime juice
1 tsp salt
1 tsp red chilli powder

Second marinade:

1 tsp ginger paste
2 tsp garlic paste
3 tbsp yogurt, whisked
½ tsp ajwain
1 tsp dried fenugreek leaves (kasuri methi)
2 drops red food colour (optional)

Gravy:

As given for seekh kabab makhani masala (see p. 44)

- Wash fish thoroughly and pat dry. Rub fish with lime juice, wash and pat dry again.
- Combine all ingredients for first marinade. Rub into fish and set aside for 30 minutes.
- Combine all ingredients for second marinade. Rub into fish. Sprinkle in gram flour, mix gently, till well blended and set aside for 30 minutes.
- Fix fish on to skewers, 1" apart, and roast in a preheated tandoor, regular oven or grill, as given on p. 3 for about 10 minutes initially, and 3-4 minutes after draining and basting with oil.
- Slip fish off skewers and set aside.
- Make a gravy as given for seekh kabab makhani masala (see p. 44) and mix fish into it.

Note: Make sure you buy food colour of a reputed brand.

Variation: The tikka can also be served as a snack without the gravy, accompanied with onion rings and lime wedges.

IMLI MACHCHI TIKKA

TAMARIND-FLAVOURED FISH KABAB

Serves: 6

350 gms boneless sole, cut into 3" pieces
Refined oil for basting

First marinade:

½ tsp salt
½ tsp white pepper powder
2 tsp white vinegar

Second marinade:

3½ tbsp tamarind
1½ tsp grated jaggery
½ cup hung yogurt, whisked (see p. 4)
½ tsp red chilli powder
½ tsp cumin powder
½ tsp garam masala powder
¼ tsp asafoetida powder (hing)
½ tsp salt

- Wash fish thoroughly and pat dry.
- Combine all ingredients for first marinade. Rub into fish and set aside to marinate for 30 minutes.
- Soak tamarind and jaggery in 1 cup warm water for 30 minutes. Extract pulp and set aside.
- Whisk hung yogurt in a bowl and add tamarind pulp and remaining ingredients for second marinade. Mix till well blended.
- Drain fish and add to bowl. Rub marinade into fish and set aside for about 1 hour.
- Fix fish on to skewers, 1" apart, and roast in a preheated tandoor, regular oven or grill, as given on

p. 3 for about 8 minutes initially, and 3-4 minutes after draining and basting with oil.

- Slip fish off skewers and serve hot with mint chutney (see p. 8).

Variation: **Imli Paneer Tikka** can be made in the same way. Cut paneer into 1½" cubes and proceed as given above.

GARLIC PRAWNS

Serves: 8

1 kg jumbo prawns
1½ tbsp maize flour (makki ka atta)
Melted butter for basting

Marinade:

1 tbsp garlic paste
2 green chillies, seeded and crushed
2 tbsp white vinegar
1½ tbsp poppy seeds (khus-khus)
1 tsp salt

- Shell prawns, retaining their tails. De-vein, wash thoroughly and pat dry.
- Combine all ingredients for marinade. Rub into prawns and set aside for 2 hours.
- Add maize flour to bowl and mix to blend thoroughly.
- Fix prawns on to skewers, 1" apart, and roast in a preheated tandoor, regular oven or grill, as given on p. 3 for about 10 minutes initially, and 2-3 minutes after draining and basting with melted butter.
- Slip prawns off skewers and serve hot.

TANDOORI SALMON

Serves: 6

1 kg boneless salmon, cut into 3" cubes
Olive oil for basting

First marinade:

3 tbsp lime juice
½ tsp salt
2 tsp black pepper powder

Second marinade:

1 cup hung yogurt, whisked (see p. 4)
1 tsp salt
4 tsp garlic paste
5 green chillies, seeded and chopped
2 tsp chopped fresh dill (sua bhaaji)
4 tbsp olive oil

- Wash fish and pat dry.
- Combine all ingredients for first marinade. Rub into fish and set aside for 30 minutes.
- Combine all ingredients for second marinade in bowl. Drain fish and add to bowl. Mix till fish is well coated with marinade and set aside for about 1 hour.
- Fix fish on to skewers, 1" apart, and roast in a preheated tandoor, regular oven or grill, as given on p. 3 for about 10 minutes initially, and 2-3 minutes after draining and basting with olive oil.
- Slip fish off skewers and serve hot, accompanied with onion rings.

STIR-FRIED POMFRET

Serves: 3-4

800 gms pomfret fillets
Refined oil for shallow-frying

First marinade:

1½ tsp salt
4 tbsp malt vinegar

Second marinade:

3 tbsp tamarind
1 tsp red chilli powder
10 green chillies
1 tsp coriander powder
¼ cup chopped mint leaves
1 cup (200 gms) chopped coriander leaves

- Wash fish and pat dry.
- Combine all ingredients for first marinade. Rub into fish and set aside.
- Soak tamarind in ¼ cup hot water and extract pulp. Grind tamarind pulp with remaining ingredients for second marinade to make a smooth paste. Rub over fish and set aside to marinate for about 30 minutes.
- Heat oil in a non-stick frying pan and fry fish in batches over moderate heat on both sides till crisp and cooked through. Drain and place on kitchen paper to absorb excess oil.
- Serve hot.

Vegetarian Dishes

PANEER METHI MALAI

Fenugreek-Flavoured Creamy Cottage Cheese

Serves: 2

150 gms cottage cheese (paneer)
1½ tbsp refined oil
1½ tsp ginger-garlic paste
1 small onion, chopped
¾ tsp red chilli powder (degi mirch)
1½ tbsp garam masala powder
¾ tsp cumin powder
1 tsp salt
2½ tbsp chopped tomato
2 tbsp dried fenugreek leaves (kasuri methi)
1 tbsp butter
2½ tbsp cream

Garnish:

1½ tsp ginger juliennes

- Cut paneer into 1" cubes and set aside.
- Heat oil in a kadhai or wok. Add ginger-garlic paste and sauté for 2-3 minutes over moderate heat. Add onion and sauté for 2 minutes. Sprinkle in spice powders and salt and give it a stir.
- Mix in tomato and fenugreek leaves and sauté for a few minutes.
- Add paneer and toss gently to coat.
- Add butter and stir for 2-3 minutes.
- Mix in cream, stir for 1 minute and remove from heat.
- Serve hot garnished with ginger juliennes

TANDOORI BHARWAN KHUMB

STUFFED TANDOORI MUSHROOMS

Serves: 6-8

20 large fresh mushrooms
Melted butter for basting

Filling:

200 gms cottage cheese (paneer), grated
3 tsp chopped coriander leaves
¾ tsp salt

Marinade:

²/₃ cup hung yogurt (see p. 4)
2 tsp ginger-garlic paste
½ tsp mustard powder
2 tsp nigella seeds (kalaunji)
2 tbsp gram flour (besan), roasted
½ cup refined oil
¾ tsp salt
1 tsp turmeric powder
2 tsp garam masala powder
1 tsp red chilli paste (see p. 6)

- Remove and discard stems from mushrooms. Wash mushroom caps under running water, drain and pat dry.
- Combine ingredients for filling in a bowl and mix well.
- Scoop out centre of mushroom caps and stuff caps with filling.
- Combine ingredients for marinade in a large bowl and carefully immerse mushroom caps into marinade. Set aside for about 1 hour.
- Fix mushrooms on to skewers, 1" apart, and roast in a preheated tandoor, regular oven or grill, as given on p. 3 for 5-6 minutes initially, and 3-4 minutes after

draining and basting with melted butter.
- Slip mushrooms off skewers and serve hot with mint chutney (see p. 8).

PANEER BIRBALI

Cottage Cheese in a Cashew Nut Gravy

Serves: 3-4

150 gms cottage cheese (paneer)
2 tbsp refined oil
1 medium-sized onion, chopped
2 tbsp cashew nut paste (see p. 5)
1 tsp salt
1½ tsp white pepper powder
¾ tsp cashew nuts, broken
¾ tsp seedless raisins (kishmish)
1½ tbsp butter
⅓ cup cream

- Cut paneer into 1" cubes and set aside.
- Heat oil in a kadhai or wok. Add onion and sauté over moderate heat till light pink.
- Stir in cashew nut paste and sauté for 2-3 minutes. Add paneer, salt and pepper. Simmer gently over low heat for 3-4 minutes, stirring carefully to coat paneer.
- Mix in cashew nuts and raisins.
- Add butter and stir for about 2 minutes.
- Add cream, stir for a minute and remove from heat.
- Serve hot.

TANDOORI FRUIT CHAAT

TANGY TANDOORI FRUIT

Serves: 3-4

100 gms apples
100 gms guavas
100 gms pineapple
100 gms sweet potato, peeled
Refined oil for basting

Marinade:

1½ tsp red chilli powder (degi mirch)
¾ tsp cumin powder
1 tsp chaat masala (commercial)
¾ tsp garam masala powder
¾ tsp coriander powder
¾ tsp black salt (kala namak)
¾ tsp dried fenugreek leaves (kasuri methi)
¾ tsp ajwain
1 tsp salt
1 tbsp corn flour
2 tbsp yogurt
1 tsp malt vinegar
2 tsp refined oil

Garnish:

½ tsp chaat masala

- Wash fruit and sweet potato, drain and pat dry. Cut into 2" cubes.
- Combine ingredients for marinade. Mix in fruit and sweet potato and set aside for 30 minutes.
- Fix fruit and sweet potato on to skewers, 1" apart, and roast in a preheated tandoor, regular oven or grill, as given on p. 3 for about 5 minutes initially, and 2-3 minutes after draining and basting with oil.

- Slip fruit and sweet potato off skewers and arrange on a serving platter. Sprinkle chaat masala and serve hot with plum chutney.

SUBZ DIWANI HANDI

MIXED VEGETABLES IN A RICH GRAVY

Serves: 2-3

3 tbsp refined oil
1 tsp mint leaves + 1 tsp coriander leaves, ground
6½ tbsp cashew nut paste (see p. 5)
$^1/_3$ cup chopped carrots
$^1/_3$ cup chopped French beans
$^1/_3$ cup shelled green peas
$^1/_3$ cup chopped potato
$^1/_3$ cup cauliflower florets
$^1/_3$ cup cubed cottage cheese (paneer)
1½ tsp green cardamom powder
1½ tsp white pepper powder
1 tsp salt
$^1/_3$ cup fruit cocktail (commercial)
2½ tbsp butter
Scant ½ cup cream

- Heat oil in a kadhai or wok. Add mint-coriander paste and stir for 1 minute over moderate heat.
- Add cashew nut paste. Stir to blend and mix in all vegetables and paneer. Cover pan and cook for 5-8 minutes, till tender, stirring occasionally.
- Sprinkle in spice powders and salt and mix gently.
- Stir in fruit cocktail and cook for 1 minute.
- Add butter and sauté for 2 minutes. Pour in cream, give it a stir and remove from heat.

TANDOORI SALAD

Serves: 3-4

2 medium-sized onions
2 medium-sized green bell peppers
2 medium-sized tomatoes
100 gms peeled pineapple
100 gms cottage cheese (paneer)
Refined oil for basting

Marinade:

2¼ tbsp yogurt
¾ tsp red chilli powder (degi mirch)
¾ tsp cumin powder
1½ tsp garam masala powder
¾ tsp black salt (kala namak)
1½ tsp chaat masala (commercial)
1 tsp salt
¾ tsp dried fenugreek leaves (kasuri methi)
¾ tsp ajwain

Garnish:

½ tsp chaat masala

- Peel onions. Remove and discard seeds of bell peppers and tomatoes. Cut vegetables, pineapple and paneer into 2" cubes and set aside.
- Combine ingredients for marinade in a bowl. Mix in vegetables, pineapple and paneer and set aside for about 1 hour.
- Fix vegetables, pineapple and paneer on to skewers, 1" apart, and roast in a preheated tandoor, regular oven or grill, as given on p. 3 for about 5 minutes initially, and 2-3 minutes after draining and basting with oil.
- Slip vegetables, pineapple and paneer off skewers and arrange in a serving platter. Sprinkle chaat masala and serve hot.

The Moti Mahal Cookbook

MALAI PANEER TIKKA

Cottage Cheese Kabab

Serves: 2

250 gms cottage cheese (paneer)
2 tbsp refined oil

Marinade:

2½ tbsp cashew nut-cheese paste (see p. 5)
1 tsp ginger-garlic paste
¾ tsp white pepper powder
1 tsp salt
¾ tsp green cardamom powder
1½ tbsp cream
¾ tsp ajwain

Garnish:

¾ tsp chaat masala (commercial)

- Cut paneer into 2" cubes and set aside.
- Combine ingredients for marinade. Mix in paneer and set aside for about 30 minutes.
- Gently fix paneer cubes on to skewers, 1" apart, and roast in a preheated tandoor, regular oven or grill, as given on p. 3 for 5 minutes initially, and 2-3 minutes after draining and basting with oil.
- Slip paneer off skewers and arrange on a serving platter. Sprinkle chaat masala and serve hot.

Variation: **Malai Paneer Tikka Masala:** Make a gravy as given for seekh kabab makhani masala (see p. 44) and mix the cooked tikka into it.

PUDINA TANDOORI PHOOLGOBHI

MINT-FLAVOURED TANDOORI CAULIFLOWER

Serves: 3-4

4 medium-sized cauliflowers
3 green cardamoms
1" stick cinnamon
4 cloves
5 black peppercorns
2 tsp salt
Oil for basting

Marinade:

3 tbsp yogurt
1½ tsp red chilli powder (degi mirch)
1½ tsp garam masala powder
1½ tsp cumin powder
¾ tsp black salt (kala namak)
1 tsp salt
¾ tsp chaat masala (commercial)
¾ tsp coriander powder
¾ tsp dried fenugreek leaves (kasuri methi)
2 tbsp ginger-garlic-mint paste (see note)

- Cut cauliflowers into large florets. Wash thoroughly and drain.
- Bring a pan of water to boil with whole spices and salt.
- Remove pan from heat and add cauliflowers. Set aside for 10 minutes.
- Drain cauliflowers and plunge into iced water. Drain when cool and pat dry.
- Combine ingredients for marinade, rub into cauliflowers and set aside for 1 hour.
- Fix cauliflower florets on to skewers, 1" apart, and roast in a preheated tandoor, regular oven or grill, as

given on p. 3 for 8-10 minutes initially, and 2-3 minutes after draining and basting with oil.

• Slip cauliflower off skewers and serve hot with mint chutney (see p. 8).

Note: To make **ginger-garlic-mint paste** soak 6 cloves of garlic and a 1" piece of ginger in water for 5 hours. Chop roughly and grind with 2 tbsp mint leaves to a smooth paste.

NADRU KABAB

Lotus Stem Kabab

Serves: 4

750 gms lotus stem (kamal kakdi)
2 medium-sized potatoes, boiled, peeled and roughly chopped
4 tsp chopped ginger
6 green chillies, chopped
2½ tbsp chopped coriander leaves
1¼ tsp salt
2 tbsp yellow chilli powder
1 tbsp garam masala powder
A pinch of green cardamom powder
A pinch of nutmeg powder (jaiphul)
2 tbsp breadcrumbs
Refined oil for deep-frying

Garnish:

½ tsp tandoori masala (see p. 7)

- Scrub lotus stems thoroughly under running water, peel and slice on the slant. Boil lotus stems in water to cover till tender. Drain and set aside till cool.
- Place lotus stems in a processor and process to make a fine mince. Add potatoes, ginger, green chillies and coriander leaves and process well.
- Sprinkle in salt, spice powders and breadcrumbs and process to make a smooth paste.
- Divide mixture into 14 equal portions. Moisten your hands and shape into balls. Press balls between your palms to shape into flat, round kababs.
- Heat oil in pan and deep-fry kababs in batches over moderate heat, till golden brown on both sides. Drain and place on kitchen paper to absorb excess oil.
- Sprinkle with tandoori masala and serve hot with mint or garlic and chilli chutney (see pp. 8 and 9).

The Moti Mahal Cookbook

TANDOORI ALOO TIKKA

Tandoori Potato Kabab

Serves: 2

2 medium-sized potatoes
¾ tsp refined oil + extra for basting

Marinade:

1 tbsp yogurt
1½ tsp red chilli powder (degi mirch)
¾ tsp cumin powder
¾ tsp garam masala powder
¾ tsp coriander powder
¾ tsp black salt (kala namak)
½ tsp salt
1½ tsp ginger-garlic paste
¾ tsp ajwain

Garnish:

¾ tsp chaat masala (commercial)

- Wash potatoes, peel, cut into 1½" cubes and parboil till half-cooked. Drain and set aside till cool.
- Combine all ingredients for marinade in a bowl. Mix in potatoes and set aside for about 30 minutes.
- Fix potatoes on to thin skewers 1" apart, and roast in a preheated tandoor, regular oven or grill, as given on p. 3 for 5-6 minutes initially, and 3-4 minutes after draining and basting with oil.
- Heat ¾ tsp oil in a frying pan and fry tikka over moderate heat till crisp.
- Drain, sprinkle with chaat masala and serve hot.

MAKAI KABAB

CORN KABAB

Serves: 4

100 gms baby corn
A pinch + 1 tsp turmeric powder
500 gms corn kernels, boiled
250 gms cottage cheese (paneer), grated
1 tbsp chopped green chillies
1 tsp ginger-garlic paste
2 tbsp chopped coriander leaves
1 tsp Kashmiri red chilli powder
1 tsp garam masala powder
1 tsp tandoori masala (see p. 7)
1¼ tsp salt
Refined oil for basting

- Clean baby corn and wash. Cook baby corn in boiling water with a pinch of turmeric till tender. Drain and set aside.
- Mix corn kernels and paneer in a bowl. Add remaining ingredients except baby corn and oil. Mix well with your hand.
- Divide mixture into 12 equal portions and shape into balls. Moisten your hands and fix the balls on to skewers, shaping them into 2" long kababs along the length of the skewers.
- Roast in a preheated tandoor, regular oven or grill, as given on p. 3 for 7-8 minutes initially, and 3-4 minutes after draining and basting with oil.
- Slip kababs off skewers and insert a baby corn at the end of each kabab.
- Serve hot with mint chutney (see p. 8).

PALAK MAKAI MALAI

SPINACH AND CORN IN A CREAMY GRAVY

Serves: 2

200 gms spinach
1½ tbsp refined oil
3 tbsp chopped onion
1½ tsp ginger-garlic paste
⅓ cup corn kernels
¾ tsp garam masala powder
¾ tsp cumin powder
¾ tsp red chilli powder (degi mirch)
1 tsp salt
1 tbsp butter
2½ tbsp cream

Garnish:

1 tbsp chopped coriander leaves

- Pluck spinach leaves and discard stems. Wash spinach leaves in several changes of water, drain and chop roughly.
- Boil spinach in ½ cup of water for 3-4 minutes. (Do not cover pan while boiling.) Drain spinach and set aside till cool. Blend to a smooth paste.
- Heat oil in a kadhai or wok. Add onion and sauté for 2-3 minutes over moderate heat. Add ginger-garlic paste and stir for 2 minutes.
- Blend in spinach and sauté for 2 minutes. Stir in corn kernels and sauté for 2-3 minutes longer. Sprinkle in spice powders and salt, and give it a stir.
- Add butter and stir for a minute. Mix in cream, stir for a minute and remove from heat.
- Serve hot, garnished with coriander leaves.

SUBZ MELONI KABAB

Mixed Vegetable Kabab

Serves: 2

1/3 cup chopped carrots
1/3 cup chopped French beans
2/3 cup chopped potato
1½ tsp chopped coriander leaves
6 medium-sized mushrooms, chopped
¾ tsp garam masala powder
¾ tsp cumin powder
¾ tsp chaat masala (commercial)
½ tsp salt
¾ tsp chopped cashew nuts
¾ tsp seedless raisins (kishmish)
¼ cup breadcrumbs
2½ tbsp crushed vermicelli (seviyan)
Refined oil for deep-frying

- Boil all vegetables in water till tender. Drain and cool.
- Grind vegetables to make a thick paste. Mix in spice powders, salt, nuts and raisins.
- Divide into 12 portions and shape into balls.
- Sprinkle breadcrumbs on a plate and roll kababs in breadcrumbs to coat. Sprinkle crushed vermicelli on another plate and roll kababs in crushed vermicelli to coat thoroughly.
- Heat oil in a kadhai or wok and deep-fry kababs in batches over moderate heat till golden brown. Drain and place on kitchen paper to absorb excess oil.

KHATTA MEETHA PANEER SHAHI TIKKA

SWEET AND SOUR COTTAGE CHEESE KABAB

Serves: 3-4

400 gms cottage cheese (paneer)
2 tsp mango chutney (see p. 10)
Refined oil for basting

Ground to a fine paste:

5 tbsp chopped unripe mango
2 sprigs curry leaves
2 green chillies

Marinade:

1 tbsp ginger-garlic paste
1 tsp salt
1 tsp chaat masala (commercial)
1 tsp red chilli powder
¾ tsp corn flour
3 tbsp refined oil

Garnish:

1½ tbsp chopped coriander leaves

• Cut paneer into 2" cubes. Make an incision in the centre without disjointing the cubes.
• Mix mango chutney into ground paste. Reserve a quarter of the paste and stuff paneer cubes with remaining paste.
• Combine ingredients for marinade and mix in reserved ground paste. Gently mix in paneer cubes, coating well and set aside for 1 hour.
• Fix paneer cubes on to skewers 1" apart, and roast in a preheated tandoor, regular oven or grill, as given on p. 3 for 7-8 minutes initially, and 3-4 minutes after draining and basting with oil.
• Garnish with coriander leaves and serve hot with any chutney of choice.

BHARWAN SHIMLA MIRCH

STUFFED BELL PEPPERS

Serves: 3-4

2 yellow bell peppers, cut into half with pith and seeds removed
3 red bell peppers, cut into half with pith and seeds removed

Filling:

1 cup cracked wheat (dalia)
1 cup bean sprouts
2 tomatoes, finely chopped
3 tbsp finely chopped spring onions
1 tbsp dried parsley
1 tbsp dried mint leaves
4 tbsp olive oil
4 tbsp lime juice
1 tsp salt
1 tsp freshly ground black pepper
1$^1/_3$ cups yogurt

Garnish:

5 green olives, sliced

- Soak cracked wheat in cold water for 30 minutes. Drain and squeeze out all water.
- Place wheat in a bowl, and mix with remaining ingredients for filling, except yogurt. Set aside.
- Cook bell pepper shells in salted water for about 5 minutes. Drain and pat dry.
- Mix yogurt into bowl containing cracked wheat.
- Fill into bell pepper shells, garnish with olives and serve at room temperature.

The Moti Mahal Cookbook

KHATTA MEETHA BAINGAN

Sweet and Sour Aubergine

Serves: 3-4

500 gms medium-sized aubergines (baingan)
1 cup tamarind
2 cups + 5 tbsp refined oil
4 dried red chillies
1 tbsp nigella seeds (kalaunji)
1 sprig curry leaves
5 medium-sized onions, finely chopped
2 tsp salt
2 tbsp sugar

- Wash aubergines and pat dry. Make a slit at the base of aubergines to come three-quarters of the way up.
- Soak tamarind in 2 cups of warm water for 30 minutes. Press tamarind pulp through a strainer into a bowl. Discard residue in strainer.
- Heat 2 cups of oil in a kadhai or wok and fry aubergines in batches, for 5-7 minutes over moderate heat. Drain and place on kitchen paper to absorb excess oil.
- Heat 5 tbsp oil in another kadhai or wok and sauté red chillies, nigella seeds and curry leaves for 1 minute over moderate heat.
- Add onions and sauté over moderate heat, till light brown.
- Pour in tamarind pulp and bring to boil. Lower heat, sprinkle in salt and sugar and give it a stir.
- Add fried aubergines and 1 cup of water, stir gently to coat aubergines with spices and simmer over low heat for about 10 minutes.
- Remove from heat and serve hot with steamed rice.

PINDI CHANA

RAWALPINDI CHICKPEAS

Serves: 5-6

2 cups chickpeas (kabuli chana)
1 tsp salt
1 tbsp cumin seeds
2 tsp shredded ginger
1 large potato, boiled, peeled and cubed
5-6 tsp refined oil
1 tbsp ghee

Marinade:

½ tsp garam masala powder
1 tbsp coriander powder
1 tsp red chilli powder
1½ tbsp dried pomegranate seeds (anardana), coarsely ground
1 tsp salt

Garnish:

2 green chillies, slit and seeded
1 medium-sized tomato, cut into quarters
1 small onion, cut into rings
1 lime, cut into wedges

- Wash chickpeas and place in a bowl with 1 tsp salt. Add water to cover and set aside to soak overnight.
- Drain chickpeas and rinse in several changes of water.
- Place chickpeas in a pressure cooker with 1 litre of water and cook under pressure for 40-45 minutes. Open cooker when cool, drain chickpeas and reserve cooking liquid.
- Combine ingredients for marinade in a bowl. When chickpeas are cool, add to bowl containing marinade with cumin seeds, ginger, potato and oil. Mix well and set aside for 3 hours.

- Transfer contents of bowl to a kadhai or wok and place over low heat. Add 1 cup of reserved chickpea liquid. Simmer over low heat for 30 minutes.
- Remove from heat and spoon into a serving bowl. Drizzle hot ghee on top and garnish with chillies, tomato, onion and lime.

ZIMIKAND KABAB

YAM KABAB

Serves: 3-4

1½ kg yam (zimikand)
1 tsp finely chopped green chillies
1 tsp finely chopped ginger
1½ tsp salt
1 tsp white pepper powder
1 tsp red chilli powder
1 tsp chaat masala (commercial)
1 tsp finely chopped coriander leaves
½ cup breadcrumbs
¾ cup refined oil

- Peel yam and wash well. Plunge into boiling water and cook for about 10 minutes, till tender. Drain thoroughly and grate fine. Squeeze out all excess water.
- Mix remaining ingredients, except oil into yam. Mix well and divide into 8 equal portions. Shape into round patties.
- Heat oil in a frying pan. Shallow-fry kababs in batches over moderate heat till crisp and golden brown on both sides. Drain and place on kitchen paper to absorb excess oil.
- Serve hot with mint chutney (see p. 8).

MAKHANI CHANA DAL

HUSKED BENGAL GRAM IN A RICH SPICY GRAVY

Serves: 3-4

1 cup husked Bengal gram (chana dal)
½ tsp turmeric powder
1½ tsp salt
3 cloves
1 bay leaf (tej patta)
¼ tsp asafoetida powder dissolved in 1 tbsp water
½ cup makhani gravy (see note)
1 tbsp butter

Tempering:

2 tbsp refined oil
1 large onion, chopped
2-3 whole dried red chillies
1 tsp red chilli powder
1 tsp coriander powder
1 tsp garam masala powder

Garnish:

2 tsp chopped coriander leaves
1 lime, cut into wedges
2 green chillies, sliced and seeded

- Clean gram and wash in at least 3 changes of water.
- Drain gram and place in a pan over moderate heat with turmeric, salt, cloves, bay leaf and 4 cups of water. Bring to boil, reduce heat to low and cook for about 15 minutes.
- Remove from heat and set aside.
- Heat oil for tempering in a deep pan and sauté onion over moderate heat till brown.
- Add red chillies and stir-fry for 30 seconds.

- Sprinkle in remaining ingredients for tempering and stir for another 30 seconds.
- Pour in asafoetida water and stir for 30 seconds.
- Drain gram and add to pan. Sauté for 2-3 minutes.
- Stir in makhani gravy and sauté for 2-3 minutes longer.
- Add butter and stir till it melts
- Serve hot garnished with coriander leaves, lime wedges and green chillies.

Note: To make ½ cup makhani gravy use the recipe given for murgh makhani (see p. 22), using a quarter of the quantities given there.

DAL HARDILLI

SAFFRON-FLAVOURED LENTILS

Serves: 4-6

1¼ cups pigeon peas (arhar/toover dal)
1 tsp + ½ tsp turmeric powder
1½ tsp salt
2 tbsp butter
1 large onion, quartered
1½ tsp black cumin seeds (kala jeera)
1 tbsp red chilli powder
5 saffron strands soaked in 1 tbsp cream

- Wash dal thoroughly under running water. Soak in cold water for about 30 minutes.
- Bring 2 litres of water to boil in a heavy-based pan. Drain dal and add to pan. Bring to boil again and remove any scum formed on top.
- Lower heat, add 1 tsp turmeric, cover pan and cook for 10-12 minutes, till dal is tender. Stir in salt and remove from heat.
- Melt butter in another pan over moderate heat. Add onion and sauté till brown.
- Sprinkle in remaining turmeric, cumin seeds and chilli powder and stir. When cumin seeds start to splutter, pour contents of pan into cooked dal.
- Place dal over moderate heat and simmer for 2-3 minutes. Pour saffron-cream into dal and stir for a minute.
- Serve hot with rice.

Rice

ZAFRANI BIRYANI

Saffron-Flavoured Chicken Biryani

Serves: 4-6

1 kg chicken without skin
2½ cups basmati rice
1 + 1 bay leaves (tej patta)
2 + 8 green cardamoms
2 + 8 cloves
1 tsp + 1 tsp salt
¾ cup unsalted white butter
2 black cardamoms
4 x 1" sticks cinnamon
1 tsp mace blades (javitri)
1½ tsp black cumin seeds (kala jeera)
1 medium-sized onion, sliced
2²⁄₃ tsp chopped ginger
2²⁄₃ tsp chopped garlic
1 tbsp red chilli powder
1¼ cups yogurt
2 tsp lime juice
1½ tsp aromatic spice mix (see p. 7)
Stiff dough made with 1½ cups refined flour (maida) and ¼ cup water

Saffron-flavoured yogurt:
15 saffron strands
½ cup milk
¼ cup cream
1¼ cups yogurt, whisked
2 tsp chopped mint leaves
2 tsp chopped coriander leaves

Garnish:
2 tbsp slivered, fried almonds

- Clean chicken and cut into 8 pieces. Wash thoroughly and set aside to drain.

- Wash rice and soak in water for at least 30 minutes.
- Prepare saffron-flavoured yogurt by soaking saffron in milk and cream for about 10 minutes. Mix in yogurt and mint and coriander leaves and set aside.
- Bring 4 litres of water to boil in a large pan with 1 bay leaf, 2 green cardamoms and 2 cloves. Drain rice and add to pan with 1 tsp salt. Boil for about 10 minutes till rice is half-cooked. Drain rice with whole spices and keep hot.
- Melt butter in a pan over moderate heat. Add remaining whole spices and sauté for 30 seconds. Add onion and sauté till golden brown. Mix in ginger, garlic and chilli powder and stir for about 15 seconds.
- Add chicken and 1 tsp salt and cook for 5 minutes. Stir in plain yogurt and ¾ cup water. Bring to boil, stirring continuously. Lower heat and simmer for about 10 minutes, till chicken is almost cooked.
- Stir in lime juice, taste and adjust seasoning, and remove from heat.
- Spread half the chicken in a lightly greased ovenproof dish. Sprinkle half the saffron-flavoured yogurt on top. Spread half the parboiled rice over this. Repeat layering once more. Sprinkle aromatic spice mix over the last layer.
- Place a damp cloth over the rice and cover dish with a lid. Seal with dough and place in oven preheated to 150°C for 10-12 minutes.
- Serve hot, garnished with fried almonds.

KATHAL PUNJABI PULAO

Jackfruit Pulao

Serves: 3-4

1 cup basmati rice
1 cup refined oil
1¼ cups cleaned and cubed jackfruit (kathal)
4 cloves
1" stick cinnamon
2 black cardamoms
1 tsp black cumin seeds (kala jeera)
1 bay leaf (tej patta)
1 small onion, chopped
2 tsp ginger paste
½ tsp red chilli powder
¾ tsp white pepper powder
1½ tsp salt
1 tsp aromatic spice mix (see p. 7)
Stiff dough made with 1½ cups refined flour (maida) and ¼ cup water

Garnish:

1 tsp chopped cashew nuts, fried
½ tsp chopped coriander leaves
½ tsp ginger juliennes
1 tsp sliced, seeded green chillies
1 tbsp lime juice
½ tsp mace powder (javitri)
1 medium-sized onion, sliced and fried crisp

- Wash rice and soak in water for 30 minutes.
- Heat oil in a kadhai or wok till smoking. Lower heat and fry jackfruit in batches over moderate heat till light brown. Drain and place on kitchen paper to absorb excess oil.
- Transfer oil to a heavy-based pan and place over moderate heat. Toss in whole spices and bay leaf.

When they start to splutter, add onion and sauté till golden.

- Stir in ginger paste, spice powders and salt. Cook for 3-4 minutes, stirring frequently.
- Drain rice and add to pan with 2½ cups of water. Bring to boil, lower heat, cover pan and cook for 8-10 minutes till rice is half-cooked.
- Open pan and spread jackfruit, aromatic spice mix and ingredients for garnish over rice.
- Cover pan and seal with dough. Place pan on a tava or griddle over very low heat to cook on dum for 10-12 minutes.
- Serve hot with any raita of choice.

GUCCHI BIRYANI

Mushroom Biryani

Serves: 8-10

1 kg basmati rice
100 gms large mushrooms
1½ tsp salt
1 tsp aromatic spice mix (see p. 7)
Stiff dough made with 1½ cups refined flour (maida) and ¼ cup water

Filling:

2 tbsp grated cottage cheese (paneer)
2 tsp chopped cashew nuts
2 tsp seedless raisins (kishmish)
1 tsp chopped ginger
½ tsp cumin seeds
½ tsp salt

Gravy:

½ cup refined oil
2 tsp mixed whole garam masala
1 cup ground onions
¾ cup yogurt
2 tbsp cashew nut paste (see p. 5)
2 tbsp ginger-garlic paste
½ tsp turmeric powder
1 tsp yellow chilli powder
1 tsp salt

- Wash rice and soak in water for at least 30 minutes.
- Remove and discard stems from mushrooms. Wash mushroom caps under running water. Drain and squeeze out excess water.
- Combine ingredients for filling in a bowl and mix well. Scoop out centre of mushroom caps and stuff mushrooms with filling. Set aside.

- Heat oil for gravy in a pan. Toss in whole garam masala. When it splutters, add ground onions and cook till water released from onions evaporates.
- Mix in remaining ingredients for gravy and cook for a few minutes, stirring frequently. Remove from heat and set aside.
- Boil rice in plenty of water with salt, till three-quarters done. Drain and set aside.
- Spread alternate layers (twice) of rice, mushrooms and gravy, starting and ending with rice. Sprinkle aromatic spice mix on top.
- Cover pan and seal with dough. Place pan on a tava or griddle over very low heat to cook on dum for 10-12 minutes till rice and mushrooms are tender.
- Remove from heat and serve hot with any raita of choice.

Tandoori Breads

NAAN

Makes: 8 naan

500 gms refined flour (maida) + extra for dusting
A pinch of salt
1 egg, whisked
½ tsp baking powder
1 tsp sugar
3½ tbsp milk
1½ tbsp refined oil
½ tsp nigella seeds (kalaunji)
1 tsp fennel seeds (badi saunf)

- Sift flour with salt into a thali (a flat metal plate with a 1" rim).
- Place egg, baking powder, sugar and milk in a bowl and whisk till well blended.
- Make a well in the centre of the flour and pour in egg mixture. Bring flour into well gradually and blend in. Gradually add up to 1½ cups of water, and knead to make a soft, pliable dough. Set aside for 10 minutes.
- Add oil to dough and knead and punch dough, till oil is absorbed. Cover dough with a damp muslin cloth and set aside for 2 hours to allow it to rise.
- Knead dough lightly and divide into 8 equal portions. Roll into balls and place on a lightly floured surface.
- Sprinkle nigella and fennel seeds and pat balls to flatten slightly. Set aside for about 10 minutes.
- Flatten each ball between your palms, lightly dusted with flour, and make a round disc. Stretch one end to shape into an oval teardrop.
- Place naans on a gaddi (cushioned pad) in a moderate-hot tandoor.
- Bake for 3-4 minutes and serve hot.

KHURMI NAAN

Tomato and Cheese-Flavoured Leavened Indian Bread

Makes: 8 naan

Naan dough made with 500 gms refined flour (see p. 115)
Extra four for dusting
2 tsp refined oil
1 cup tomato purée
A pinch of salt
1½ tbsp sugar
½ tsp red chilli powder
2½ tbsp grated processed Cheddar cheese

- Divide dough into 8 equal portions. Shape into balls and place on a lightly floured surface.
- Heat oil in a pan. Add tomato purée and cook for 5-7 minutes over moderate heat, till oil floats to the surface. Add salt, sugar and chilli powder and cook till reduced to a thick paste.
- Remove from heat and stir in cheese. Mix till well blended and set aside till cool
- Flatten each dough ball between your palms, lightly dusted with flour, and make a round disc. Stretch one end to shape into an oval teardrop.
- Brush tomato-cheese paste over naan.
- Cook as given for naan (see p. 115) and serve hot.

Variation: **Garlic Naan:** Make a paste of 4 garlic cloves, 2 tbsp coriander leaves and 2 tbsp water. Spread over naans in place of tomato-cheese paste.

PYAAZ KULCHA

Leavened Indian Bread with an Onion Filling

Makes: 4 kulcha

Naan dough made with 500 gms refined flour (see p. 115)
Extra flour for dusting
1½ tbsp melted butter

Filling:

1 large onion, chopped
2 green chillies, chopped
1 tbsp chopped coriander leaves
½ tsp salt

- Combine ingredients for filling in a bowl and divide into 4 portions.
- Divide dough into 4 equal portions. Shape into balls and place on a lightly floured surface.
- Slightly flatten a ball of dough to form a small disc. Place a portion of filling in centre of disc. Gather up edges of dough to cover filling completely. Press top firmly and pinch dough to seal thoroughly. Cover with a damp cloth and set aside for a few minutes.
- Flatten each ball between your palms, lightly dusted with flour, and make an 8" round disc.
- Cook as given for naan (see p. 115).
- Spread melted butter over kulchas and serve hot.

KEEMA KULCHA

LEAVENED INDIAN BREAD WITH A MINCED LAMB FILLING

Makes: 4 kulcha

Naan dough made with 500 gms refined flour (see p. 115)
Extra flour for dusting
1½ tbsp melted butter

Filling:

2 tbsp ghee
1 tbsp ginger-garlic paste
½ tsp red chilli powder
½ tbsp chopped green chillies
½ tsp salt
150 gms minced lamb
1 tsp chopped coriander leaves

- Heat ghee in a pan. Add ginger-garlic paste and chilli powder and sauté over moderate heat for about 30 seconds.
- Add green chillies and salt, and sauté till ghee floats to the surface.
- Add mince and sauté over low heat till tender and cooked.
- Sprinkle in coriander leaves, taste and adjust seasoning. Set aside till cool. Divide into 4 portions.
- Divide dough into 4 portions, roll into balls and place them on a lightly floured surface.
- Stuff and make kulcha as given for pyaaz kulcha (see p. 117), and serve hot.

Desserts

BADAAM HALWA

ALMOND SWEET

Serves: 2-3

500 gms almonds, blanched, peeled and chopped
1 cup milk
1 cup ghee
2½ cups sugar
1½ tsp green cardamom powder
¼ tsp saffron strands

Decoration:

2 silver leaves (chandi ka varq)

- In a food processor, grind almonds with a little of the measured milk to make a fine paste.
- Heat ghee in a heavy-based pan. Add almond paste and cook over moderate heat till light golden.
- Add remaining milk and sugar and cook over moderate heat for 10-15 minutes, till moisture evaporates and mixture becomes thick.
- Remove from heat and mix in cardamom powder and saffron.
- To serve cold, spread on a greased tray and allow to cool. Cut into diamonds and decorate with silver leaf.
- To serve hot, spoon individual portions on to dessert plates and decorate with silver leaf.

KESARI PHIRNI

SAFFRON-FLAVOURED MILK CUSTARD

Serves: 4

1 litre full cream milk
½ cup rice flour
1 cup sugar
A pinch of salt
²/₃ tsp green cardamom powder
4-5 drops rose water

Decoration:

¼ tsp saffron strands dissolved in 2 tsp milk
¼ cup pistachio nuts, chopped
10 pink or red rose petals
2 silver leaves (chandi ka varq)

- Place half the milk in a heavy-based pan over moderate heat and bring to a slow boil.
- Dissolve rice flour in the remaining cold milk and slowly add to hot milk, stirring continuously. Cook over very low heat, stirring constantly till mixture has the consistency of a light custard.
- Add sugar and salt and cook for 2-3 minutes, till sugar is completely dissolved. Remove from heat and set aside till cool.
- Stir in cardamom powder and rose water.
- Pour into an earthenware serving bowl and decorate with saffron milk, pistachio nuts, rose petals and silver leaves.
- Chill till set.

Glossary

ENGLISH	HINDI
Ajwain	*See note*
Almond	Badam
Aniseed	Saunf
Apple	Seb
Asafoetida	Hing
Aubergine/brinjal	Baingan
Bay leaf	Tej patta
Bell pepper/capsicum	Shimla mirch
Bengal gram	
–Flour	Besan
–Husked	Chana dal
–Whole	Kala chana
Black beans/gram	
–Husked	Urad dal/urad dhuli
Black cumin seeds	Kala jeera/shah jeera
Black pepper	Kali mirch
Black salt	Kala namak
Bread	Double roti
Brinjal/aubergine	Baingan
Butter	Makkhan
–Clarified	Ghee
Capsicum/bell pepper	Shimla mirch
Cardamom	
–Black	Badi elaichi
–Green	Hari/chhoti elaichi
Carrot	Gaajar
Cashew nut	Kaju
Cauliflower	Phoolgobhi
Chicken	Murgh

Chilli	Mirchi
–Dried red	Sookhi mirch
–Green	Hari mirch
Cinnamon	Dalchini
Clove	Laung
Coconut	
–Copra (dry)	Kopra
–Fresh	Nariyal
–Milk	Nariyal ka doodh
Coriander	Dhania
–Fresh/leaves	Hara dhania
Corn	Makkai
–Cob	Bhutta
–Flour	Makki ka atta
Cottage cheese	Paneer
Cream	Malai
Cucumber	Kheera/kakdi
Cumin seeds	Jeera
–Black cumin	Kala/shah jeera
Curd/yogurt	Dahi
Curry leaf	Kari patta
Dill	Sua bhaaji
Egg	Anda
Fennel seeds	Badi saunf
Fenugreek	
–Dry leaves	Kasuri methi
–Fresh leaves	Methi bhaaji
–Whole seeds	Methi dana
Fish	Machchi/machchli
French beans	Fransbin
Garlic	Lasun
Ginger	
–Dry	Saunth
–Fresh	Adrak
Green peas	Mattar

Groundnut/peanut	Mungphali
Honey	Madh/shahad
Jackfruit	Kathal
Jaggery	Gur
Lentil	Dal
Lettuce	Salad ke patté
Lime	Limbu/nimbu
Lobster	Barra jhinga
Mace	Javitri
Mango	Aam
–Powder	Amchur
Melon seeds	Magaz
Milk	Doodh
Mince	Keema
Mint	Pudina
Mushroom	Dhingri/ khumb
Mustard	
–Oil	Sarson ka tel
–Seeds	Sarson/rai
Mutton	Gosht
Nigella	Kalaunji
Nutmeg	Jaiphal
Oil	Tel
Onion	Pyaaz
Papaya	Papeeta
–Unripe	Kaccha papeeta
Peanut/groundnut	Mungphali
Peppercorn	
–Black	Kali mirch
–White	Safaid mirch
Pickle	Achaar
Pigeon peas	Arhar/toover
Pineapple	Annanas
Pistachio nuts	Pista
Plum	Aadu bukhara

Pomegranate	Anar
–Dry seeds	Anardana
Pomfret	Chhamna/paplet
Poppy seeds	Khus-khus
Potato	Aloo
Prawn	Jhinga
Pumpkin	
–White	Doodhiya
–Red/yellow	Kaddu
Raisin	
–seedless	Kishmish
Rice	Chaval
–Flour	Chaval ka atta
Rose water	Gulabjal
Saffron	Kesar/zafran
Salt	Namak
Screwpine flower/	
vetiver essence	Kewda
Sesame seeds	Til
Silver leaf	Chandi ka varq
Spinach	Palak
Spring onion	Hara pyaaz
Sugar	Cheeni/shakkar
Tamarind	Imli
Tomato	Tamater
Turmeric	Haldi
Vermicelli	Sevian
Vetiver/screwpine	
flower essence	Kewda
Vinegar	Sirka
Walnut	Akhrot
Wheat	Gehun
–Broken/cracked	Dalia
–Plain/refined flour	Maida
–Wholewheat flour	Atta

| Yam | Zimikand |
| Yogurt | Dahi |

Notes:

Ajwain: It is an umbelliferous plant which grows in India and the Far East. It is sometimes referred to as carom seeds, and belongs to the same family as the Ethiopian bishop's weed and English lovage.

Olives, parsley: These ingredients have no Indian names but are readily available in speciality shops.

Index

CHUTNEYS
Aam ki chutney (Mango chutney) 10
Coriander chutney (A blend of fresh coriander) 8
Lasun aur mirch chutney (Garlic and chilli chutney) 9
Mint chutney (The famous Moti Mahal chutney) 8
Peanut chutney 9
Till aur tamater ki chutney (Sesame and tomato chutney) 11

COTTAGE CHEESE
Imli paneer tikka (Tamarind-flavoured cottage cheese
    kabab) 77
Khatta meetha paneer shahi tikka (Sweet and sour cottage
    cheese kabab) 97
Malai paneer tikka (Cottage cheese kabab) 89
Malai paneer tikka masala (Cottage cheese kabab in a
    rich tomato gravy) 89
Paneer birbali (Cottage cheese in a cashew nut gravy) 85
Paneer methi malai (Fenugreek-flavoured creamy cottage
    cheese) 83

DESSERTS
Badaam halwa (Almond sweet) 121
Kesari phirni (Saffron-flavoured milk custard) 122

LENTILS
Dal gosht (Lamb with lentils) 48
Dal hardilli (Saffron-flavoured lentils) 104
Makhani chana dal (Husked Bengal gram in a rich
    tomato gravy) 102
Pindi chana (Rawalpindi chickpeas) 100

MUTTON AND LAMB
Badamé shami kabab (Lamb kabab with almonds) 43
Chatpatté pudina chaamp (Tangy lamb chops) 52
Dal gosht (Lamb with lentils) 48

Gosht lababdar (Lamb in a rich creamy gravy) 46
Gosht pasanda masala (Mutton escalope in a tomato gravy) 50
Kasuri gosht kabab (Fenugreek-flavoured lamb kabab) 53
Pasanda kabab (Lamb escalope) 57
Seekh kabab gilafi (Lamb kabab with a vegetable coating) 54
Seekh kabab makhani masala (Lamb kabab in a rich tomato gravy) 44
Spicy lamb steaks 56

RELISHES
Irani raita (Iranian relish) 15

RICE
Gucchi biryani (Mushroom biryani) 111
Kathal Punjabi pulao (Jackfruit pulao) 109
Zafrani biryani (Saffron-flavoured chicken biryani) 107

SEAFOOD
Dahi mahi machchi (Fish in a yogurt gravy) 70
Dhania pomfret tandoori (Coriander-flavoured tandoori pomfret) 64
Garlic prawns 77
Goan fish curry 61
Imli machchi tikka (Tamarind-flavoured fish kabab) 76
Machchi musallam (Spicy baked fish) 62
Machchi tikka masala (Fish kabab in a rich tomato gravy) 74
Stir-fried pomfret 79
Tandoori lobster – 1 67
Tandoori lobster – 2 68
Tandoori salmon 78
Tandoori trout 66
Tangy fish fry 65

Tava machchi (Pan-fried fish) 72

SOUPS
Palak shorba (Cumin and burnt garlic spinach soup) 16
Rice soup 17

SPICE POWDERS
Aromatic spice mix 7
Garam masala powder 6
Tandoori masala 7

TANDOORI BREADS
Garlic naan (Garlic-flavoured leavened Indian Bread) 116
Keema kulcha (Leavened Indian bread with a minced
    lamb filling) 118
Khurmi naan (Tomato and cheese-flavoured leavened
    Indian bread) 116
Naan (Leavened Indian bread) 115
Pyaaz kulcha (Leavened Indian bread with an onion
    filling) 117

VEGETABLES
Aubergine
Khatta meetha baingan (Sweet and sour aubergine) 99

Bell pepper
Bharwan Shimla mirch (Stuffed bell peppers) 98

Cauliflower
Pudina tandoori phoolgobhi (Mint-flavoured tandoori
    cauliflower) 90

Corn
Makai kabab (Corn kabab) 94

Palak makai malai (Spinach and corn in a creamy
     gravy) 95

Lotus stem
Nadru kabab (Lotus stem kabab) 92

Mixed vegetables
Subz diwani handi (Mixed vegetables in a rich gravy) 87
Subz meloni kabab (Mixed vegetable kabab) 96
Tandoori fruit chaat (Tangy tandoori fruit) 86
Tandoori salad 88

Mushrooms
Tandoori bharwan khumb (Stuffed tandoori
     mushrooms) 84

Potato
Tandoori aloo tikka (Tandoori potato kabab) 93

Spinach
Palak makai malai (Spinach and corn in a creamy
     gravy) 95

Yam
Zimikand kabab (Yam kabab) 101